CAMRA
at 40

CAMPAIGN
FOR
REAL ALE

CAMRA
BOOKS

D1434101

CAMPAIGN
FOR
REAL ALE

Published by Campaign for Real Ale Ltd.
230 Hatfield Road
St Albans
Hertfordshire AL1 4LW

www.camra.org.uk/books

First published 2011

ISBN 978-1-85249-300-4

A CIP catalogue record for this book is available
from the British Library.

Printed and bound in the United Kingdom by
CPI Group (UK) Ltd, Croydon, CRO 4YY

Head of Publishing: Simon Hall
Project Editor: Katie Hunt
Book Designer: Dale Tomlinson

CONTENTS

CAMRA CELEBRATING **40** years OF CAMPAIGNING

A CAMRA celebrates its 40th year, should we look back on our successes, of which there are many? Should we congratulate ourselves for getting this far – a feat no one expected when Messrs Hardman, Makin, Mellor and Lees started the Campaign for the Revitalisation of Ale (thankfully shortened to the Campaign for Real Ale) in March 1971? Or should we look ahead at work still to be done, the challenges still to be met and how we might need to adapt to achieve our objectives? At this milestone in our history, I believe that we should do of all of these things, and that is the purpose of this book.

The contributions in the following pages provide a variety of fascinating perspectives on the Campaign and its work – from both within and outside the organisation. Some of the contributors look back at their experiences in CAMRA, others challenge the perceived CAMRA orthodoxy. In my opinion, that is no bad thing, as if our early activists had accepted the status quo and not challenged the onward march of keg beer, then we wouldn't be here now. Despite the prevailing wisdom of CAMRA being stuck in the 1970s, the truth is that we have adapted to meet challenges as they have arisen, and with a considerable degree of success. Now, with more than 130,000 members, we can seek to set the agenda in ways that we would never have thought possible even 10 years ago.

I trust that this book gives you enjoyment and food for thought in equal measure.

Colin Valentine

COLIN VALENTINE
CAMRA National Chairman

Michael Parkinson

One of the problems of growing old is that things are never as good as they were. On the other hand there are few organisations – and CAMRA is one – whose dedicated ambition is to enable us to say that there are pubs and there are beers which we can sample without feeling the slightest bit nostalgic. It is true I have never found one better than Barnsley Bitter but, on the other hand, I have drunk one or two brews which have prevented me from being suicidal about the lack of the beer of my youth. CAMRA stands for quality and common sense. It should have a representative in Parliament. If it took over the country it might just steer us away from the precipice.

SIR MICHAEL PARKINSON CBE is a broadcaster, author and journalist. His chat show *Parkinson* ran on BBC television and then ITV from 1971 to 1982 and from 1998 to 2007. With his son Nick, he runs the Royal Oak in Paley Street, Maidenhead, Berkshire.

Roger Protz

No room for complacency

IF I had a pound for every time the national chairman of CAMRA had opened the annual members' meeting with the warning 'There's no room for complacency' I wouldn't be rich but I'd certainly have around thirty pounds more in my bank account. If it seems downbeat to open a book that celebrates the Campaign's fortieth anniversary with that same warning, I merely point you in the direction of Mike Benner's and Andrew Pring's contributions to underscore the point. In some ways, CAMRA has never been stronger. Membership stands at 130,000, making it the biggest single-issue consumer movement in the world. Real ale shows the only growth – albeit small – in a beer market that's in overall sharp decline. The British may be drinking less beer but they are undoubtedly drinking better beer. The choice today is remarkable, with once-dead styles such as Porter and India Pale Ale plucked from the grave to stand alongside new interpretations – golden ales, fruit beers and oak-aged beers to name but three – on the bars of the nation's pubs. The number of breweries nudges ever closer to 900, the greatest number since the 1940s and four times as many as when CAMRA was founded in 1971.

But the storm clouds are not on the horizon – they hang ominously overhead, ready to rain on our fortieth parade. As Mike Benner stresses, pubs are closing at an alarming rate of knots and every closed pub is one less outlet for draught beer. Living, breathing, natural cask-conditioned beer needs a pub cellar to reach maturity and go through the arcane rituals of 'tapping and spiling' before it's pulled to the bar and into your waiting glass. The gains made in recent years, principally the growth of the micro-brewery sector discussed here by Julian Grocock of SIBA, could go into reverse unless we can stop the dreadful cull of pubs. Melissa Cole, in a perceptive contribution that rightly praises the way in which pub owners have made their outlets more welcoming to women, will also raise a few hackles with her view that Britain may have been 'over-pubbed' and the trade will become leaner and fitter when it emerges from its current travails. It's a widely-held view in the brewing industry but not one that will be shared by many CAMRA members. In the past few months I have travelled to former industrial heartlands – South Wales, Lancashire and West Yorkshire – and seen the impact that pub closures have had on communities where thousands have seen their jobs disappear and along with them the small but important pleasure of drinking good beer in pleasant community pubs. Greg Mulholland, a whirlwind of energy on behalf of the pub in Parliament, details the way in which governments of all persuasions have consistently failed to protect the beleaguered pub in their rush to cosy up to supermarkets. The high street giants use their massive marketing power to sell alcohol as a 'loss leader' to lure customers into their stores. In a more positive vein, he outlines a series of proposals – drawn up in concert with CAMRA – to save community locals, while John Longden of Pub is the Hub shows how his organisation is ready to help with detailed plans on community buy-outs of pubs, turning them into co-operatives or small businesses run by shareholders.

CAMRA marked its twenty first birthday with a book, *Called to the Bar*. It was a retrospective volume that recalled the founding of the Campaign and its early struggles with the Big Six national brewers, who attempted to foist keg beer and a poor imitation of lager on to the hapless public. Twenty years later, this book attempts something different (though several references to Watneys Red Barrel from contributors suggests the infamous keg beer that helped kick-start CAMRA has not been forgotten among older drinkers). Rather than looking back down the well-trod path of the 1970s, we are attempting to focus on the current state of the beer and pub trades and how consumers can help determine their future. There have clearly been important gains in recent years. Jeff Evans, who deserves great praise for his work in almost single-handedly reviving the bottled beer sector, and Zak Avery show the enormous improvements in packaged and imported quality beers. Des de Moor describes how beer has developed a language of appreciation that puts it on a par with wine, while Paula Waters and John Bishop trace the development of national and local beer festivals. The festivals have not only watered 'beer deserts' but also improved choice for drinkers and – to the surprise of once-hostile publicans – helped boost pub business.

CAMRA is often seen as one of those eccentric British institutions that is revered at home but is impossible to export, like croquet and the House of Lords. But its impact

among beer lovers world-wide should not be underestimated.
Julie Johnson, a distinguished American beer writer,
contributes a thoughtful essay on how the Campaign has
influenced the rise of craft brewing in the United States
even if many of their end products are not kosher by our
definition. Similar change is underway in Australia and
New Zealand, which have closer ties with the Old Country
and where many British brewers have moved to practise
their craft and influence domestic practitioners. The British
contribution should not be underestimated. When I visited
Coopers in Adelaide, brewers of celebrated Sparkling Ale
and Stout, I admired the company's impressive new but
highly traditional brewhouse and asked if it had been built
in Australia. Glenn Cooper looked puzzled and replied:
'Of course not – we got it from Burton-on-Trent. If you want
to make proper pale ale you have to use Burton equipment.'

There are, however, worrying threats to cask beer in Britain.
As Andrew Pring points out, the global brewers are aware
that demand for their lacklustre lagers and 'smooth-flow' keg
ales are in decline and they are searching for new products to
boost flagging sales. A major report on the global brewers in
the weekly business magazine the *Economist* in May said that
in response to sluggish sales further takeovers and mergers
could be expected. According to the magazine, the $52 billion
merger in 2008 between Anheuser-Busch in the US – the
owner of Budweiser – and the Brazilian-Belgian group InBev
'saved a fortune...cost-cutting through mergers will have
boosted global brewers' profits by $3 billion over the five years
to 2012, estimates Credit Suisse.' The combined international
market share of the top four international brewers – AB InBev,
Heineken, SABMiller and Carlsberg – grew by 22 per cent in

volume in 1998 to nearly 50 per cent in 2010, according to the *Economist*. That's a frightening thought – half the world's beer brewed by just four companies. The savings made from mergers could send these cash-rich giants on the takeover trail and that puts successful small brewers in the spotlight. In February 2011, Molson Coors, a Canadian-American group that occupies the former Bass breweries in Burton-on-Trent, bought Sharp's brewery in Cornwall for £20 million. Sharp's has a substantial portfolio of cask beers but Molson Coors only mentions its leading brand, Doom Bar. Molson Coors becomes enraged if commentators suggest it will reduce Sharp's portfolio and eventually close the Cornish brewery. But the proven track record of the global brewers is to concentrate production in a few large, centralised units close to the motorway network.

The ink was scarcely dry on the Sharp's deal when Anheuser-Busch, the American arm of AB InBev, bought the Chicago craft brewer Goose Island for $39 million. Goose Island also has a large beer range, including Belgian-style ales and a stout aged in bourbon casks. Whether they survive remains to be seen. It's more likely that AB will home in on Goose Island's main brands, IPA and Honker's Ale. The main – and worrying – message to emerge from these takeovers is: If you can't brew it, buy it. Molson Coors' expertise lies in Carling lager while AB is famous/infamous (take your pick) for Budweiser, a lager brewed with a large proportion of rice. If sales of these brands are not buoyant then the temptation will be to acquire cask beers that are showing growth. Heineken UK, Britain's biggest brewer as a result of buying Scottish & Newcastle, will be aware of the success of its Caledonian Deuchars IPA and may look to add to its cask portfolio. On the other hand, AB InBev and Carlsberg seem lost causes in Britain: AB InBev has put up for sale Draught Bass and Boddingtons, once jewels in the cask crown, while Carlsberg has closed the Tetley brewery in Leeds in order to concentrate on its lagers brewed in Northampton. Iconic may be an over-used term but it surely applied to Tetley: as one of its former draymen told me, 'If you close Tetley's you might as well close Leeds' but the historic importance of the brewery and its beer seems lost on the Danes.

The all-too-evident threat to the British pub and the worrying possibility of takeovers that could threaten successful small breweries underscore the message: 'There's no room for complacency'. CAMRA will continue to campaign as the champion of the beer drinker. It needs more members and a bigger voice in the parliaments and assemblies of Britain and Europe. But, at the age of 40, while not resting on our laurels, we can raise a glass and cheer the remarkable achievements of the past forty years that has seen real ale revive beyond the wildest dreams of its founders. Choice and diversity have never been greater. More than 200 beer festivals a year offer a profusion of ales: no longer just Mild and Bitter but a variety of styles beyond imagination in the dark days of the 1970s. So, without a hint of complacency, there is much to celebrate. Drink deep and consider that forty years is no more than a rehearsal for the Big 50 in 2021. Keep the faith!

ROGER PROTZ joined CAMRA in 1976. A journalist and author, he has edited *What's Brewing*, is currently editor of the *Good Beer Guide*, and has written many books about pubs and beer.

The pub
in
peril

Mike Benner

Saving the British Pub

*To write of the English Inn is to write of England itself...
as familiar in the national consciousness as the oak and
the ash and the village green and the church spire.*

THOMAS BURKE, 1930

AS you've bothered to start reading this article, I suspect that, like me, you love pubs. Together, we love them because each and every one of them is unique, and stepping over the threshold of a pub for the first time is always met with excitement, anticipation and expectation.

We're not alone. The pub features high in surveys on British icons. It's always named as one of the top tourist attractions. Everyone, it seems, regards community pubs with affection, a treasured possession to be handed down to the next generation. Pubs are undoubtedly one of the oldest and most important of our social institutions.

In the past three years, though, 4,000 pubs have rung time and closed their doors for ever. As I write, nearly 30 pubs are still shutting up shop every week. How did we get here? How can it be that this essential British institution, widely touted to be at the heart of our communities and an essential amenity for the good of society and personal well-being, appears to be slipping away from us at this alarming rate? In 1979 there were 70,000 pubs. Now there are barely more than 50,000 and we Brits now sup 16 million fewer pints a day than we did in the first year of the Thatcher government.

CAMRA recognised early on in its 40-year life that pubs were essential to the future of real ale. If there were no pubs, where would we enjoy our national drink? Former Chairman Chris Hutt wrote a whole book, *The Death of the English Pub*, on the subject back in 1973, in which he challenged how the spirit and fabric of English pubs was being destroyed by big business. Now, in 2011, much of our campaigning effort centres on promoting community pubs and lobbying government and industry to protect them.

There are many factors that have led to the decline of the community pub. As a population, our habits have changed, tastes have changed and more people now drink wine when they used to drink beer, the staple product of pubs. We stay at home more, choosing the comfort of our favourite armchair and the company of the *EastEnders* cast over a bar stool in a smoke-free pub. 70% of alcohol is now consumed outside the pub environment, mostly at home. The decline of manufacturing and British industry has changed towns and villages beyond recognition, drastically affecting the viability of pubs in many areas. Pubs have faced massive competition from other leisure pursuits, be it bowling, cinema, eating-out or retail parks (which for many seem to be treated as places of leisure rather than necessity). The price of beer in pubs has rocketed due to increasing business costs and outrageous increases in beer duty, which large supermarkets can absorb or pass back to suppliers, but pubs can only pass on to customers. The cost of compliance with an endless stream of regulations has increased dramatically. Last, but by no means least, the anti-competitive behaviour of the big pub companies has crippled many pub businesses through high rents and beer prices, making it impossible for tenants to invest and to make a reasonable living.

So, it would be fair to say that all is not rosy in the beer garden. On the positive side though, despite these incredible pressures and the 'perfect storm' as it's been called, that pubs face, they are still with us and they keep on bouncing back. The reason for that is because society and individuals would be much worse off if pubs disappeared. Pubs play two essential roles in society: firstly they provide a regulated and, crucially, a sociable place for folk to enjoy alcohol, and secondly – and this is their main role – they provide a meeting place for people from all walks of life, rich and poor, to come together as part of a unique social network. At the bar, it matters little which school you went to or what car you are driving; everyone is equal. In 'Pubs and Places', published by the Institute of Public Policy Research in 2009, pubs featured highest of any location in a survey asking people where they get together with others in their neighbourhood. Quite clearly, pubs are the glue that holds many communities together.

It's more than this, though. Pubs also bring authenticity and heritage to communities often dominated by global retail. They may often sit behind our homogenised high streets, but they remain at the heart of those communities, despite these transformations. There is evidence that many British people are fed up with globalism and big business that bring little to their community. We are wiser now to the fact that a new supermarket or retail chain moving in always means small local businesses move out, taking jobs, values and traditions with them. The perception of community pubs is that they don't fall into this category. Owned by a local brewer or as a free house, they are part of the history of communities, built and run by local people and typically injecting £80,000 into the local economy.

The good news is that, finally, after many years of campaigning, our political leaders seem to recognise the essential role of well-run community pubs. In the dying weeks of the last Labour government, John Healey, having been appointed as the first ever Pubs Minister, put forward his 12-point plan, heavily influenced by CAMRA, to save Britain's pubs. It was an impressive list of initiatives that included reforming the beer tie and banning the use of restrictive covenants as a means to stop pubs being run as pubs when they are sold (a deeply damaging and anti-competitive practice). It was as if all CAMRA's Christmases had come at once.

Sadly, it was not to be and the May 2011 election meant CAMRA had to knock on a few new doors to convince the Coalition government that community pubs desperately need their support. Thankfully, they listened. David Cameron announced that his was to be a 'pub friendly' government and a new Community Pubs Minister was appointed. This provides a new champion in government and CAMRA has enjoyed significant successes in the last 12 months alone, including a ban (of sorts) on the below-cost selling of alcohol, a commitment to reform the tie if the industry proves itself unable to do so itself, a community right-to-buy in the Localism Bill, and a commitment to consult to ban restrictive covenants.

In spite of these steps forward, there are still a few giant strides required if we are truly going to see a sea-change in the fortunes of Britain's crisis-hit community pubs. Other organisations have joined us in calling for a policy framework from government to support community pubs and reward well-run pubs that genuinely contribute to the well-being of society. To get there, we must see a change in approach to excise duty on beer, which remains the most important product for most pubs. There has been a 35% increase in beer tax since 2008 and this, alongside higher VAT rates, is contributing to the decline. We must see a tax policy that recognises that beer is a low-strength, responsible product and we must see a tax regime that benefits community pubs over supermarkets.

Finally, as we head into the next 40 years of campaigning, we must not fall into the trap being set by many people in the pub industry who claim that thousands more pubs need to close in order to create a viable marketplace for those that remain. This is the economics of doom and to accept it will spell the end of pubs in the lives of hundreds more British communities. CAMRA's own research shows that few people would bother to walk or drive to a pub that is more than a few minutes from their front door. If their local closes, they simply stop using pubs regularly and once that happens they are most unlikely ever to do so again.

Every community needs a pub. CAMRA will continue to fight to achieve this and to ensure a level playing field in which they can operate so they can bring pleasure and well-being to millions of British people.

MIKE BENNER is CAMRA's Chief Executive.

John Longden

Taking the helm at the village local

THE local village pub is a great British institution, called the 'heart of England' by Samuel Pepys. Today, however, there is a tidal wave of change sweeping through society and all local services. Through Pub is The Hub we try to encourage pub diversification to support the changing needs of local customers in their communities by providing essential services.

It is not too surprising that there are few businesses that emotionally matter more to people in their neighbourhoods than their own local, more it seems than the shop or the post office. Over the past 10 years there has been a domino effect on the closure of services that support the community. Small rural settlements in particular are often home to vulnerable groups experiencing deprivation and therefore the role of the community in providing support in these areas has never been more needed.

Community ownership and operation of pubs has slowly created interest as being a model for retaining some local pubs in villages and neighbourhoods and the aim is wherever feasible to help some pubs remain at the heart of their communities.

However, important key decisions need to be faced up to, such as how is the pub actually going to be run by the community and can the pub really be a viable and sustainable business in the long term? Especially after the first year, a business needs to pay its way and make a surplus for reinvestment in the future. It should always be borne in mind that if a pub is facing closure or alternative use because it is no longer profitable, can the community add that extra bit of sparkle? Perhaps it can, because the people who constitute the community are also the customers who feel strongly about a loss of facilities.

The first important step in any community pub venture is the need to decide the most appropriate ownership model for those involved. A purchase of a freehold can be achieved using methods that include co-operative ownership or a private limited company. On the other hand, renting or leasing may give an opportunity of running the pub before it's bought but without the need to raise as much capital finance by allowing funds to be spent on improving the trading areas, kitchen and living accommodation, which may well have been neglected. An option to purchase the pub at a later date may also be built into a lease, as many communities still find it a challenge to get a sufficient number of locals interested and get the financial support and muscle to actually be able to make it work. After the initial excitement, the main challenge has been for everyone to ensure that the pub can remain a sustainable business in the future. We encourage communities to include much-needed services if they possibly can, such as allotments, support for the elderly or whatever is felt to be essential in the local community.

While anecdotal evidence and knowledge from Mike Clayton, who is responsible for the community side of Pub is the Hub, suggests there are probably around 30 existing community pubs trading, we are currently assisting more than 50 communities who are in the process of considering and deliberating on the merits of taking over their neighbourhood pub. The range of models varies according to the personal circumstances and objectives of the villagers. For example, at the Dykes End in Reach, Cambridgeshire, Bryan Pearson and the community formed a company limited by guarantee and then pledged the freehold to their parish council who subsequently signed a long lease to an approved operator. But a local management group remains to oversee the community objectives and they still retain the freehold for control and peace of mind in the future.

The Raven Inn at Llanarmon-yn-Ial in Denbighshire took a lease on the property from the owner, while the villagers of the New Inn at Shipton Gorge in Dorset agreed a nine-year lease on a fixed rental terms of their local, with the help of Palmers of Bridport, their local brewer. At the George & Dragon in Hudswell, North Yorkshire, where the pub had been closed since 2008, the community formed a co-operative society to enable them to buy and refurbish the pub. It opened in February 2010 and is now the centre of social activity in the community, with a wider range of local services including a shop, local library and allotments.

The village of Ennerdale Bridge, Cumbria, is made up of only around 200 dwellings, having lost its shop, post office and bus service. After raising funds from 182 members, the pub – the Fox & Hounds – re-opened under community ownership in April 2011. Nearby, the villagers of Crosby

Ravensworth are hoping to be able to re-open the Butchers Arms in a similar fashion.

As is well known, in 2003 not only did a group of villagers and other friends set up a co-operative in Hesket Newmarket, Cumbria, to acquire their own local pub, the Old Crown, but a second, additional co-operative was later formed to run the traditional Hesket Newmarket Brewery, at the rear of the property, which must be one of the few co-operative breweries with its own local tap room and range of ales. HRH The Prince of Wales has now made two visits to the brewery to support this marvellous initiative, one in 2004 to help launch the CAMRA 'Save the Pub' brochure. Greg Smith, the brewery manager, confirms that the brewery continues to do well, which is good in a very competitive environment for local cask beers.

Some community pubs have also been acquired by an individual or groups of benefactors in the village who then put in their own local manager to run the pub for the community. This is not altogether surprising when estate agents feel a house in a village with a pub is often worth 10 per cent more than a house in a similar village without one.

Many communities are surprised at the diverse range of practical and legal issues that are involved in running a pub as a business. Unlike customers in any other retail trade, pub customers are often seeking more than merely the product that is being sold. It could be companionship, local advice, romance, sympathy or entertainment – possibly all at the same time, combined with some excellent beer, good food and supportive local services. As any good licensee knows, you ignore any of these combinations at your peril.

As any licensee can also testify, communities need to be prepared for long hours and lots of hard work but the results can be worth it, probably more as a sense of well-being in their local area for residents rather than the actual financial returns. It is also encouraging to see that even the larger pub companies such Punch Taverns and Enterprise Inns have recently supported communities to establish their own pub, either with investment, signage and decoration or operational advice. As Bob Neill, Minister for Community Pubs, commented in a recent forward to a community pamphlet, referring to Henrik Ibsen, the Norwegian playwright, 'A community is like a ship: everyone ought to be prepared to take the helm'. Perhaps some well-run community pubs will help define local distinctiveness and a special sense of place, which is the way most people support their communities in the first place. Believing in themselves and trying to bring back facilities that may directly affect their lives is an admirable motivator.

JOHN LONGDEN is Chief Executive of Pub is the Hub, which was launched in 2001 by HRH Prince Charles, the Prince of Wales, as part of his Business in the Community initiative.

John Humphrys

Playing the What if? game is always great fun...
if only because no-one can ever be proved wrong.
What if Gavrilo Princip's gun had jammed when
he pulled the trigger in Sarajevo in 1914 and
Archduke Franz Ferdinand had lived to a ripe
old age? What if Britain had voted to pull out of
the European Common Market? What if CAMRA
had never existed? Maybe that's not on quite
the same scale as world wars and momentous
political events, but who knows whether we'd
still be able to drink a pint of decent beer in a
British pub without it? Speaking for myself,
as someone who is old enough to remember
when Watneys Red Barrel seemed on the point of
world domination, I'm rather glad we don't have
to face that possibility. We owe them a round.

JOHN HUMPHRYS is a broadcaster, journalist and author.
He presents the BBC Radio 4 *Today* programme and
Mastermind on BBC television and is a former presenter
of the BBC's *Nine O'Clock News*.

Taking the fight to Parliament

Greg Mulholland

Time for government to save the British pub

CAMRA champions issues that are as relevant today as they were at the time of its conception, 40 years ago. The Campaign has been successful not only in changing the course of beer history and saving and then transforming the availability of real ale, but in campaigning for reforms to pub licensing hours, fairer systems of excise duty and small brewers rate relief.

In terms of British beer and the depth and breadth of great local beer up and down the country, things could scarcely be better. We have wonderful new breweries opening all the time, brewing some of the best beer this country has seen. Yet there is as much need for CAMRA as there ever was, and the biggest threat is now not to real ale, our great national drink, but to the great national institution to properly enjoy it in: the pub.

As Chair of the Parliamentary Save the Pub Group, I am used to life at the front end of this campaign and work very closely with and alongside CAMRA, championing the interests of community pubs up and down the country, a highlight being the tabling of the most signed Early Day Motion in the current Parliament, EDM 210, which pays tribute to the importance of the pub, but also calls on the government to implement policies to protect well-run community pubs.

However, there is much still to do to safeguard the future of community pubs. There are several key areas that need to be addressed to ensure the future of the British pub. I have outlined three key areas that need to be addressed – greater protection for pubs in planning law; reform of the beer tie; and lastly proper recognition, through taxation, of the importance of pubs taking on the supermarkets. The frustration, it seems, in trying to make pro-pub progress in all three areas is that governments seem unwilling to take on big, influential companies – pub owning companies, supermarkets and developers – their trade associations and the power of their lobbying power, when all too often, these companies and their practices are the reasons that pubs are shutting.

CAMRA members and pub campaigners have all heard the statistics about how many pubs are shutting; but it is not just about overall figures. The pubs closing in greatest numbers are urban and suburban pubs away from town and city centres. Large town-centre vertical drinking establishments, pub restaurants and idyllic country pubs that serve food will survive even through these hard times, but the danger is that our most special and truly unique pubs will become a thing of the past – many being backstreet locals and neighbourhood pubs. These are predominantly owned by the big pubcos and breweries. These are the easiest to claim as 'unviable', the easiest for unscrupulous developers to target, the easiest to get closures approved by local councils, the easiest to ignore campaigns to save them. We are increasingly seeing supermarkets, developers and other companies 'predatory purchasing' pubs due to their lack of protection, sometimes colluding with the pub owner, be they a big (and indebted) pub company or unscrupulous individual, greedily cashing in their 'asset' despite the fact the pub has been around much longer than they have and is still wanted by the local community who surely do – or should – have some 'moral ownership' of it. It is time that was recognised in the planning system.

Enough is enough. It is time to stop it being so easy for big companies and developers to ride roughshod over the views of local communities and those actually behind the bar, running our pubs. It is time for the government to turn the often-heard warm words into concrete action.

Planning

The first area of government action required is changes to planning law. Quite simply, according to planning law, the pub isn't important. It can be changed overnight to a restaurant or café without any process or consultation and amazingly it can be perfectly legal to demolish a pub without planning permission. It also is perfectly legal to close a pub even when it is both profitable and wanted by the community it serves. As well as being wrong, this is absurd and it is a national scandal that profitable, wanted pubs are closing every week.

If the government is serious about saving and preserving pubs, then the thing that has to happen quickest is reform of planning law. No community public house should be given change of use or be allowed to be demolished without planning permission and it is time that that should include genuine community consultation and a proper, independent viability study. If that were introduced, we would not see anything like the number of pubs closing every week that we currently do, because it would no longer be easy for their owners to try to cash in when times are hard, sacrificing years of community history and heritage for the sake of a fast buck.

The Save the Pub group recently launched a new planning charter, which highlights the key areas where reform is needed to protect pubs in the planning process. I hope the government will listen to this. It cannot say on the one hand it values the pub, then do nothing to stop those who seek to close pubs even when they are wanted and profitable.

Beer Tie

The second key area that needs addressing is the desperate need for reform of the beer tie. In the past, there has been something of a rosy relationship between the big players in the pub trade and I think that some in the trade thought that MPs could be fobbed off or hoodwinked, but successive Business Select Committees have done their public duty and exposed the sorry reality of what has happened to the pub industry since the Beer Orders to the pub sector. The picture the committee painted is one all too familiar to the thousands of tenants struggling to make a living and the many former tenants who have lost their business because of a business model that had become so skewed as to make it impossible for them to succeed. The committee made clear that the situation is seriously unfair and unsustainable.

Yet how many in this strange industry we call the pub trade are still saying there is no need for action, no need for regulation? 'Leave it to the market', they say. 'There is plenty of competition' so they say. Is it 'competition' where sometimes all the pubs in one area are owned by the same two or three companies with the same leases? Where the consumer has to pay over the odds for a pint because of the excessive price the tenant is forced to pay? What sort of free market is that? What sort of free market means that local brewers can't get their beer into local pubs at a price worth brewing it at or often not at all? In this twisted system, profitable and popular pubs are closed to cut company debt. What sort of economic sense is that? How would people feel if a landlord got into debt through irresponsible borrowing then tried to recoup this by selling a popular pub? So why is it all right for some larger company to do this, to trade our community pubs like commodity shares?

We could only have real competition in the pub sector if every single pub were a free house, competing against every other pub, all buying their beer and other products from whomsoever they wished. While that may not be realistic or even desirable, the truth is that anything else is itself a distortion of pure competition. So let's stop this nonsense of trying to use economic theory to justify what has happened to the old tied system that has ended up in the hands of property speculators calling themselves pub companies (in some cases whether they brew beer or not).

The Select Committee and the government have been clear and specific. The new Codes of Practice must include a genuine free-of-tie option, accompanied by an open market rent review and a provision for licensees to offer a guest beer outside of the tie. In the event that the pub companies fail to meet these criteria, the government is committed to intervene and implement a statutory industry code of conduct. No company code published so far offers a genuine free-of-tie option and few fully offer a guest beer option.

The history is clear. The pubcos have already been subject to three select committee inquiries and have had over six years to implement an adequate voluntary code. At the moment, they still seem unwilling or perhaps unable to do what has been very specifically asked of them. Indeed, it seems that the truth is that the pubco business model now can only survive if they continue to be allowed to take more from each pub that is reasonable or sustainable. In short, the question facing ministers is: Do they want to save the pub – or save the pubcos? It really is one or the other.

Levelling the Playing Field

The final point that needs addressing is that of the differential between the price of beer in the pub and that in supermarkets, which creates a uneven playing field for hardworking landlords, who are expected to compete with these prices. The government recently introduced a ban on selling alcohol below duty plus VAT. There is not actually a ban on below-cost selling, however, as it does not take into account the production element of any given alcoholic drink. The Save the Pub Group supports CAMRA in wanting to see a ban that includes duty plus VAT plus production, introduced as a licensing condition. CAMRA estimates this would come in at about 35 to 40p a unit for beer. It is important to note that this would be a floor price rather than an artificial minimum price, which would have perverse consequences. This would be a significant step forward in levelling out the playing field for pubs.

The idea of implementing a lower duty rate on draught beers sold in pubs is another way in which the disparity between supermarket and pub prices could be addressed, or indeed a specific rate of duty on real ale specifically.

A move like this would create further encouragement for people to drink in their local pubs, as a result doing more to ensure the long-term future of well-run community pubs. Currently the government says European law does not allow this, but we believe there are ways that this could be explored.

It is time that there were clearer guidelines for the community contribution made by local pubs to be reflected in their business rates, another way to positively recognise the contribution that pubs make to their communities.

Conclusion

The sad fact is that ministers of successive governments, despite the warm words about the pub, still don't get it. There is much a truly pub-friendly government can and must do. So, if the current government is serious about saving the pub, indeed if it is serious about the Big Society, it must properly recognise the vital role that local pubs play in communities – rural, suburban and urban – up and down the country. Yet not only is the lack of protection for pubs in planning law and the distortion of the market via the dominance of the big pub companies and supermarkets anti-community and anti-Big Society, but it is also anti-business. That is because allowing owners to selfishly shut a pub against the wishes of the local community, and often against the wishes of whoever is actually running the pub, means the end of that small business, the jobs it creates and the contribution it makes to the local economy, often for a one-off windfall for one individual or company, the greedy owner cashing in for development. That simply cannot be right and we will continue to push the government, at all levels, to accept the obvious principle that it is wrong for any profitable, wanted pub to be allowed to close against the wishes of the community. So far this is a message that government ministers are simply not getting. It is one that the Save the Pub Group will continue to communicate as loud as we possibly can.

So we need reform of the beer tie, reform of planning law and innovative ways of both tackling below-cost selling in supermarkets and using the tax system to demonstrate the worth of the community pub. Such reforms would be opposed by the big pub-owning property companies who want to continue to make decisions about pubs in their 'estate' simply to suit their shareholders' interests, by supermarkets keen to continue to have absolute power over pricing as well as the right to buy and close pubs against the wishes of communities and by developers who want to continue to see pubs as a soft target for making a fast buck. But they would be supported by all who truly care about the future of the British pub.

The big question, therefore, is will they, or will this government fall into the old cosy relationship with the big pubcos and brewers, and indeed the supermarkets and developers and decide that doing nothing is, as ever, so much easier than actually taking action to introduce bold reform and save the pub. The Save the Pub Group will continue to work alongside CAMRA to push them to have the courage to take the action that they can and must to take, to achieve real change to protect our important national institutions.

GREG MULHOLLAND is MP for Leeds North West, Chair of the All Party Parliamentary Save the Pub Group, CAMRA's Parliamentary Campaigner of the Year and a leading campaigner on beer and pub issues.

Colin Dexter

Colin's contribution is lines from
A E Housman's poem *A Shropshire Lad*:

Say, for what were hop-yards meant?
Or why was Burton built on Trent?
Full many a peer of England brews
Livelier liquors than the muse.
And malt does more that Milton can
To justify God's ways to man.

COLIN DEXTER is the creator of *Inspector Morse*.

Iain Loe

The Campaign goes to Europe

WHILE CAMRA has been active in campaigning at a national level in Britain, as well as in the corridors of power of the devolved Scottish Parliament and Welsh Assembly, we have not forgotten that much legislation that affects the beer drinker and pubgoer now emanates and is based upon Directives that are issued by the uropean Commission.

Great Britain joined what was then the Common Market in 1973 – just two years after CAMRA was founded. And we have been putting our views across to Brussels ever since. As in all lobbying, the earlier you get your voice heard and your viewpoint noted the better. Ideally this means making contact with Commission officials well before any proposed piece of legislation is put forward for consideration by Parliament and the Council of Ministers.

Surprisingly, this can be easier than is often supposed. This is especially true if you can be seen to be putting forward helpful proposals or information that can make the job of the Commission officials easier. Some of the earliest forays to Brussels by CAMRA were in the late 1970s and early 1980s.

This was when the implications of EU directives threatened the future of the traditional brewery tie. The members of what was then called CAMRA's Monopolies Committee (subsequently the Economics, Industry and Government Committee) made an early trip to Brussels where they found themselves in discussion with a Commission official whose duties were concerned with the 'Abuse of Dominant Position'. Where Britain was concerned, that meant the tied house system.

Over the years these trips have become more frequent and, with the opening of the Channel tunnel and the Eurostar, far easier than when a journey involved train, ferry and at least one overnight stop.

Today, when an issue is identified – excise duty or VAT, competition issues or ingredients listing – the relevant Directorate General, department and official can be identified, a phone call made or an e-mail sent, and a meeting set up. With more member states joining and the work of the Commission increasing it may not be as easy to quickly obtain a meeting with an official as it was in the early 1980s. So it may be easier if, rather than just representing a single nation view, CAMRA can bring a broader, more transnational view to the table.

It was with this in mind that CAMRA formed the European Beer Consumers Union (EBCU) in 1990, with similar national beer consumer groups from The Netherlands and Belgium. EBCU has now grown to cover 12 countries in Europe and continues to look to expand. So we can now approach the Commission and its officials as a European-wide consumer body rather than one just from Britain.

It can also sometimes be useful to build alliances with other industry or consumer groups on particular issues.

Lobbying alongside groups such as the British Beer and Pub Association and SIBA for reform of the Excise Duty Directives, for instance, can bring benefits for the beer consumer as well as the brewer.

While continuing to lobby Commission officials, CAMRA does not forget to get its message across to members of the European Parliament. Over the years the Parliament has continued to flex its political muscle and seek further powers. Members of the European Parliament are keen to take up issues on behalf of their constituents. Ever since the first elections for the Parliament in 1979, CAMRA has asked parliamentary candidates questions on the key issues of concern to the beer drinker and pub-goer and, if they were elected, to follow up to see that they carry out their promises. In recent elections, working with colleagues in EBCU, CAMRA has produced manifestos and asked potential MEPs to sign up to a charter for beer drinkers' rights. Each organisation has contacted candidates in their own country with copies of the manifesto. EBCU holds an annual reception in Brussels for MEPs and Commission officials to follow up these approaches and to reinforce the key issues about which we feel strongly.

The European Parliament holds regular plenary sessions at their home in Strasbourg but much of the work is done via committees that cover key subject sectors and in the political group meetings both held in Brussels. It is also in Brussels where the MEPs have offices and where the Commission resides.

Lobbying in Europe is by its very nature long and drawn out – although there can be occasions where a rapid response is needed to halt some daft piece of legislation coming into being. Back in the 1990s the Guest Beer Right for lessees of the national brewers, introduced in the wake of the 1989 Monopolies and Mergers Commission report into the Supply of Beer, came under attack from Brussels as it was felt that it contravened article 30 of the Treaty of Rome. The argument went that because the guest beer had to be cask-conditioned ale it created a barrier to trade for breweries in other EU countries because their brewers did not produce cask beer and so could not benefit from the opening up of the British market. The European Commission issued its challenge to the guest beer after a complaint from a British lager importer.

Unfortunately, for the Commission, the challenge was issued at the end of July 1996 just before they went off for a month's holiday. A few days later, at the Great British Beer Festival at Olympia, hundreds of CAMRA volunteers were wearing 'Hands off our guest ales' badges to launch a campaign to save the provision. 20,000 leaflets stating 'Brussels Threatens Real Ale Choice' had been printed, with letters written to MPs and MEPs. MEPs across the country gave their full support as they realised the threat to the many small breweries in their constituencies who had benefitted from the guest beer and whose livelihood would be harmed if the provision were banned. The campaign also received the full backing of the European Beer Consumers Union.

Working with the British government and with British MEPs, CAMRA sought to persuade Commission officials that there were plenty of continental brewers producing cask-conditioned beers. By careful lobbying CAMRA had, within six months, secured the guest beer right, with the British government adding the right of lessees to stock a bottle-conditioned beer as well to give other European brewers access to the pubs of British national brewers.

A more recent case where lobbying by CAMRA has been effective concerns the announcement by the Commission that if a member state decides to introduce a reduced rate of VAT for meals served in pubs and restaurants this would also include alcoholic drinks – a measure which if introduced by the British government would benefit the country's pubs. Before this ruling was introduced, alcoholic drinks were specifically excluded from any VAT reduction benefit. A well-argued presentation by a CAMRA delegation to the Commission was critical in securing this relaxation of the VAT rules.

Over the years CAMRA has also lobbied the Commission and Parliament on issues such as:

- listing of ingredients for alcoholic drinks (at present there is a derogation that stipulates that anything stronger than 1.2% abv doesn't have to list its ingredients)
- the ability of member states to apply a reduced excise duty for draught beer sold in pubs
- the retention of the brewery tie for smaller breweries

Increasingly, CAMRA finds itself working with the other beer consumer groups in EBCU on behalf of the beer consumer. The annual EBCU receptions for MEPs in Brussels are becoming better known and CAMRA and EBCU are acknowledged as the voice of the European beer consumer. There is still much to be done, though, when it comes to lobbying in Europe. MEPs often have a low profile in Britain. Nevertheless, they can be very useful allies for CAMRA in our fight on behalf of the consumer. If progress is to be made on key issues such as excise duty, VAT, and ingredients labelling it is essential that we engage them in the issues of concern to beer consumers and pub-goers.

IAIN LOE is CAMRA's Research and Information Manager.

Josef Tolar

The support of CAMRA in our struggle to remain out of the hands of the international predator brewers cannot be over-estimated. It was, I discovered, an organisation with sufficient influence to be listened to with respect in the Czech Republic. Whether it was government ministers, civil servants or the media, CAMRA was a name to be conjured with.

JOSEF TOLAR is the former brewmaster of Budweiser Budvar Brewery.

CAMPAIGN
FOR
REAL ALE

The people's beer

Paula Waters

On the road with the
Great British Beer Festival

THE Great British Beer Festival is a bit like Marmite: you can love it or hate it but rarely are you indifferent to it. My first experience of volunteering as a CAMRA member was at the GBBF way back in 1982 in Leeds. In those days, the event was held during September and – having finished at university and not managing to find a job – it seemed an ideal opportunity. I had one of the best weeks ever, I met some truly remarkable people, worked so physically hard that I could barely stand up at the end of the shift, and was infected by the bug of the event.

As a result of joining one of the few professions – teaching – that doesn't allow time off in September, it wasn't until 1987 that I managed to return again. The event had moved to Brighton and as the summer is the 'low season' for conference events, GBBF had switched months to August. Since then I haven't missed a festival, despite being extremely pregnant one year and having a leg entirely encased in plaster another.

Although there had been a large beer festival in Covent Garden run by CAMRA in 1975, the first under the name of Great British was held at Alexandra Palace in 1977, a tented event which, if you listen to the few hardy souls who have worked at every single GBBF since, was one of the most remarkable events on the planet. After four years it was on the move, to Leeds, then Birmingham, Brighton, Leeds, Brighton again, then finally London. Along the way, venues were burned down, demolished and put into receivership, although thankfully none of these was caused by CAMRA.

In a moment of helpfulness I said to John Norman (the festival organiser at the time) that I'd be happy to help out in any way. As a lesson in what happens if you volunteer, I was appointed Staffing Officer on the GBBF Working Party in late 1989 and have been there ever since. Although I have tried my hand at Chief Steward and Organiser, I've been back doing the Staffing role since 1999.

So what makes GBBF special? Firstly the organising committee, referred to as the Working Party. Each individual member is responsible for a huge section of the event. If they don't deliver, then the event would seriously be jeopardised and yet we still do our jobs and have fun. Over the past few years we have had stability due to the fact the venue has been fixed at Earls Court. We are all friends and take the opportunity of using the weekends when the planning meetings take place to socialise. And before anyone asks, we don't get expenses for our overnight accommodation, we pay that ourselves.

In the early days, as we moved around the country there were always new challenges: finding local suppliers for scaffolding, ice, food, accommodation, ensuring enough people from the area would come along and help staff the event, and that there was publicity to attract the punters in. When we moved to London in 1991 it made the organisation easier and growth inevitable. Accommodation for the staff was plentiful, and being in the capital, we attracted volunteers from not just across Britain but Europe and the rest of the world. The regular staff could begin to build up an understanding of the venue and plan each year to make things better. Even after all these years, I have a list entitled 'next year' that I start on day one of the event.

As the event grew, we were able to make regular deals with suppliers, and we started to build a store of equipment. At the end of the 1980s we had a garage next to CAMRA head office in St Albans that housed some banners and some hardboard, a few buckets and a couple of boxes of chocks. As London is much closer to St Albans than the other venues, it seemed logical to store things near head office. We started with a warehouse that was shared by CAMRA's fundraising group. As new innovations were brought into the event, such as cooling rather than just ice on the casks, more storage was required, and at one point we had three different warehouses. Now these have been consolidated into one and CAMRA employs three people full time to maintain and despatch the equipment to events and festivals around the country throughout the year. We even have some storage containers that are brought on to the site each year that hold specific GBBF items – a far cry from just a garage.

When I first took on the staffing job, the event in Brighton in 1990 had 455 volunteer staff in total. In 2011 there were almost three times that number. This growth is mirrored in all other areas: the number of bars and the amount of beer, the number of programmes and glasses and, of course, the number of punters in through the door. Back in the days when CAMRA organised the public food, the quantity of pies and peas used to be calculated on a daily basis. To give an idea of scale now, Marc Holmes, the current organiser, every evening reports on how much beer has been sold in terms of other CAMRA festivals: for example, three Derbys or one Worcester.

Over the years I have witnessed things that would be regarded as serious problems but I have also seen the ability of the staff to overcome them and I believe there is no problem that could not overcome. Fork lift trucks not arrived – go out and collect some; pieces of scaffolding missing – put a couple of folk in a van and go and retrieve them; massive thunderstorm that knocks out the electricity supply and floods the building – make the area safe, cordon off the flooding and carry on.

Each year we are assigned an Event Manager by the venue. It is always interesting breaking a new manager in as often we know the building better than they do. And unlike many other exhibitions it is all ours, and we know what we are doing. Other events sub-let lots of stall space to third parties who all have their own agendas and requirements. We have lots of areas to accommodate, but our festival organiser has to have a complete overview so he can make decisions and prioritise. The one thing that has astounded all these Event Managers is the fact that the entire festival is planned, organised and run by volunteers.

It is this volunteer element that confounds most outside observers. The Great British Beer Festival is huge, a flagship event for the Campaign and yet it is unpaid people, giving up their time and efforts, which is the key to its success. What is remarkable is that all this activity is done to allow each volunteer CAMRA member to share his or her love and passion of real ale with others, something that sets what is fundamentally a single issue interest group apart from any other. While many organisations run events for their members, CAMRA runs the Great British Beer Festival for the public as a means of showcasing the very best in the real ale brewing industry.

The critics don't like it for many reasons: it's too big, too impersonal, we don't sell their favourite beer, we don't have enough continental beer, we have too much continental beer, we sell cider and perry, we don't sell keg beer, there is too much music, not enough music, the wrong sort of music, there aren't enough seats – the list goes on.

I believe it is a quite remarkable event and it never fails to amaze me how all the different parts of the festival interlock and together become greater than the sum of the parts.

For those who have worked at the festival at any time in the past, you may be interested in contributing to this website, set up once again by a volunteer, to document as much as possible about past GBBFs.

www.huttoncroft.co.uk/GBBF/index.htm

PAULA WATERS has been National Chairman of CAMRA, GBBF organiser and, until 2011, a member of the Campaign's National Executive.

John Bishop

St Albans: sowing the seeds

THE first-ever beer festival in modern times took place in St Albans in December 1974 and was organised by the then all-Hertfordshire branch of CAMRA. It was not called a beer festival but a 'Beer Exhibition' but it marked the start of the kind of event that is now organised by CAMRA branches all over the country.

The St Albans Beer Exhibition sold 26 different casks of beer from 14 brewers, many of whom provided the beer for free and the beer was sold at twopence a pint – halcyon days – to an appreciative crowd of a few hundred. How things have changed! Today's St Albans Beer Festival, resurrected in 1996 to mark the 25th anniversary of CAMRA, has been going from strength to strength since and now stocks up to 350 brands of real ale while the festival attracts more than 9,000 visitors each year who drink their way through some 32,000 pints of real ale.

The organisation of a successful festival on this scale is now an all-year-round operation. The local branch, South Herts, also run the smaller but no less successful Harpenden Beer Festival. Both festivals are extensively publicised to guarantee

attendance and ensure that the festival will always be profitable and that as many of the costs as possible are covered.
To ensure that all funds raised go to CAMRA, sponsorship
and advertising at the festival and in the programme are kept
strictly in-house. The festival, however, does support local
charities with separate sponsorship schemes including 'sponsor
a cask'. If a local charity can assist the festival with organisation
or fulfilment of a sponsorship scheme, the proceeds are split.

The punters won't come through the doors in big numbers,
though, unless there's great beer (and cider and perry) on
offer, but at St Albans we don't just preach to the converted.
To entice others to the festival, we put on great entertainment
with top name acts. This helps attract potential converts and
helps with beer sales, especially on the Saturday evening,
which is the last night of the festival. A recent change of
strategy means there is less emphasis on 'weird and
wonderful' beers, with a move towards a split between
old favourites that punters can actually find in their locals
versus new and hard-to-find beers from brewers who are
known to consistently brew good beer. This has worked
well and has seen beer sales and attendances increase.

The festival doesn't hold beer back and when beer
is ready to be served it is put on sale. This ensures quick
turnover and replacement of the beer, making sure the
customer always gets an excellent pint. The use of race
spiles, which control the loss of natural CO_2 from casks, has
assisted in keeping the beer in better condition. Evaporative
cooling, although highly labour-intensive as the casks
wrapped in muslin cloth require constant spraying with
water, is surprisingly effective at cooling the casks. Space
constraints do not allow for other methods of cooling.

St Albans is a city with nearly 50 pubs, all within walking distance of the festival. CAMRA's aim with all festivals is to raise awareness of real ale and to encourage people to ask for it and drink it in their local pub. As a result, many licensees actively support the festival. One local licensee even went so far as to say that during the festival she had had her best sales of cask beer ever, proving that far from taking trade away, well-publicised CAMRA festivals can bring business into the town and compliment the work that good pubs do in promoting real ale. The organising committee know from our own research that the festival brings people from further afield to the city and that many people who visit beer festivals also visit some of the local pubs before or after their festival visit. Pub Watch in St Albans is an active sponsor of the festival and many of its members advertise in the festival programme.

Since the festival has been in existence it's probable that, along with local campaigning by CAMRA, it has acted as a catalyst by increasing demand for quality real ale in the area. Pubs in St Albans with few exceptions are now stocking a much wider range and choice of cask beer than had hitherto been the case and many now organise their own annual or seasonal beer festivals.

JOHN BISHOP is one of the organisers of the St Albans Beer Festival; www.stalbansbeerfestival.com

Tony Hadley

Thank God for CAMRA. We needed people to speak up for good British beer and we got a great consumer organisation. CAMRA is no longer blokes in green jumpers and wellies. Now great chefs are highlighting how good British beer is with food.

TONY HADLEY is the lead singer with Spandau Ballet, song writer, broadcaster and occasional stage actor. He runs the Red Rat Brewery in Suffolk.

Spreading the message

Melissa Cole

Farewell to the ladies' glass

THEY say history goes in cycles, and in the case of women and pubs, not to mention beer, this is undoubtedly true. For centuries women were the main brewers but they lost that role during the Industrial Revolution. Today's world offers greater freedoms and financial independence, allowing women to brew again and to go to the pub in greater numbers.

You could almost chart beer consumption and pub-going as a socio-economic reflection of a woman's place in civilisation's history. What is certain, however, is that women today have not only greater freedoms, but greater freedom to choose where they spend their leisure time and money. Meeting that change, the pub trade has taken great strides in making the public house accessible once more to women.

So let's start at the beginning, when women were the brewers. The Sumerians, for example, were ardent worshippers of Ninkasi, the goddess of beer. Clay tablets have been found with hymns on them praising her production of this wondrous drink. The word brewster, which means female brewer and is still a common surname, was coined in medieval times when the women not only brewed but sold nearly all the beer in England. It was also one of the only jobs acceptable for a woman who had been 'cast aside' or widowed.

Moving to more recent history, the two World Wars of the 20th century saw a huge cultural shift in the role of women, not only in industry but in society's general freedoms as well. Much as we'd like to think that the bid to attract women into pubs is a new wheeze from the pub companies and breweries, in reality, between the two major wars, brewers made a concerted bid to attract 'respectable middle-class women' into pubs, by tidying up their establishments in both urban and suburban environments by creating lounges – a development monitored by Mass Observation, a social research organisation established in 1937. Previously, pubs had been the bastion of men, who felt an entitlement to non-family leisure time due to the long hours they worked in manual and menial jobs.

This is not to say that women didn't go into pubs: quite the opposite, but they were often there only to accompany their husbands, and the majority of female drinkers in pubs were made up of working-class women over 40. Most young drinkers were only attracted to the pub if it were near to a dance hall, so they would pop out for refreshment as the dance halls were unlicensed.

But there were strongholds of outright sexism that existed during this period. For example, in Bolton, women did not order directly from the bar but frequented the parlours and lounges and were excluded from the vault and taproom. The only woman the Mass Observers of Bolton saw order a drink at the bar was a middle-class Londoner, which leads me to a personal experience of this attitude. In the early 1990s when, as a Home Counties girl, I first moved to Preston to go to university, I took the Sunday paper to the nearest pub in the backstreets of the town, stood at the bar and ordered a pint. Presumably there was something wrong with the barman's hearing as I got a half in a dreaded 'ladies' glass'. His face as I sent it back and then settled on a bar stool to spread my paper out was nothing short of priceless and it only got funnier as he made major hints that I might be more comfortable in the lounge or snug. Suffice to say I stayed put and was welcomed back as somewhat of a curiosity every time I went in. That particular pub, sadly, no longer exists, but happily neither does that attitude – which leads me on to more modern times.

I know it's not a popular view, but I believe the smoking ban has been good for the pub trade in attracting more women, and I also believe that Britain has long been over-supplied with below-par venues that cared little about customer service or product quality and have failed because they refused to move with the times. Of course, the outrageous prices that supermarkets have been allowed to charge under successive spineless governments, unethical practices by pub companies and difficult economic conditions have played more than their part. But we have to accept that the consumer has moved on and that women demand more from their leisure spend than dodgy loos and a limited range of mass-market products.

The concept that opened the floodgates was Pitcher & Piano. Twenty-five years ago P&P was the height of sophisti-cation in London and was the first place I was taken on a date in the capital. It was followed eight years later by the All Bar One concept, which grew even more quickly. The notion that a woman could go and drink somewhere with table service, that was light and airy, that she could see into before she entered, that she didn't have to suffer that embarrassing susurrus as she walked to the wrong side of the pub or, worse, panic that she'd been stood up and was stuck in the centre of a strange, hostile environment was the boon we had all been waiting for.

And then, when the smoking ban came in and pubs, free from the smell of stale tobacco, then often stank of old chip fat and urinal blocks, the light was shone on a lot of venues that women found wanting in comparison to other clean and welcoming options – one of the major reasons women abandoned beer and embraced wine.

However, all credit to the independent pub sector, with its flexibility to change its ways more quickly than corporate leviathans. It swiftly sought to embrace a new approach that would welcome women and breweries and pub companies swiftly followed. Today, you find venues such as the Jolly Butchers in Stoke Newington, North London; the Sheffield Tap; Cask Pub & Kitchen in Pimlico; the Snowdrop Inn at Lewes, East Sussex; and the White Horse in Parsons Green, south-west London, all creating environments that women want to enter, whether by themselves or with friends, and where they can experiment with beer.

In summation, to the pub industry of today I say, bravo, because when I entered that pub in Preston 18 years ago I could never have imagined that the landscape of this beloved British icon could have changed so much, embraced women customers so well, or offered so much great beer.

MELISSA COLE is a beer writer and lecturer. She is the author of *Let Me Tell You About Beer*, and writes about beer on her blog Taking the beard out of beer – a girl's guide to beer; girlsguidetobeer.blogspot.com

Catherine Maxwell Stuart

When my father started brewing at Traquair again in 1965 it was truly the dark ages for beer lovers and our traditional Scottish ales were viewed with suspicion as 'old fashioned'. Even at three shillings a bottle, it was hard to sell. I doubt my father would have continued had it not been for CAMRA and the early members who used to appear at the brewery with T-shirts proclaiming 'We're only here for the beer!' Their enthusiasm boosted my father's confidence that our ales were worth brewing and it was not long before demand had outstripped supply. CAMRA's unerring commitment to real ales has continued to help our brewery survive to this day and whereas once we were considered old fashioned now we can say we were in the forefront of the micro-brewing revolution!

LADY CATHERINE MAXWELL STUART and her family own Traquair House, Innerleithen, Scotland's oldest inhabited stately home, which dates from 1107. It has been visited by Mary Queen of Scots and Prince Charles Edward Stuart. The house has a restored medieval brewery where Traquair House Ale and other beers are produced.

Des de Moor

The language of beer:
a long journey

'The '61 Foster's [said Acton] is a really superb lager, brut,
mon, charnu, pettilante fino, pizzicato and faintly amertune.
It has that nobly fading straw-like pallor which is less a colour
than a vestment, la robe: and an aroma that is distinctly Bouverie
Street. The bouquet is a discreet cuir russe, or Old Harness.
It is urbane but quietly persuasive and with a notable wet finish...
The '61 Foster's was exhausted, but Acton found a tolerable
'62 Melbourne Bitter to go with the coffee. He assured the wine-waiter
that, though it lacked chiaroscuro and clangtint, it had a
compensatory verve, good-humoured spritzig, and almost the
panache of a pre-war Export Bass.'

CYRIL PEARL, 1964, *Pantaloons and Antics*

In some ways we haven't come that far from the days when
Australian humorist and beer drinker Cyril Pearl found
comedy in the incongruity of applying wine tasting language
to beer back in the 1960s. In Britain, a majority of people still
see beer as an everyday, unsophisticated drink best suited to
social swilling, despite its unsurpassed spectrum of flavours
and ability to match a much wider range of foods than wine.
But at least today's beer advocates are more aware of the
variety of taste experiences offered by their favourite drink,

and have found a language capable of discussing and celebrating it. Though some may still snigger or squirm at the 'pretentiousness' of talking about the taste of beer, detailed discussion of aroma, palate and finish is now an accepted part of our discourse. Informative and evocative tasting notes are a common feature of beer writing both in print and online and there are some major international websites entirely built around public rating and tasting.

Yet when the first published edition of CAMRA's *Good Beer Guide* appeared in 1974, a casual reader would have looked in vain for an indication of what the good beer it so avidly championed actually tasted like, and quite how it was different in taste, rather than in methods of production and dispense, from 'characterless' keg beer. A two-page listing of brewers summarised their entire output in the briefest of notes, ranging from 'Very highly recommended' (Brakspear) via 'Reliable' (Batham) to the notorious summation of Watney: 'Avoid like the plague', rapidly amended to 'Avoid at all costs' on the insistence of the printer.

Those requiring further detail were referred to *The Beer Drinker's Companion* by CAMRA member Frank Baillie (1973), where a section promisingly headed 'The Flavour of Beer' asserts that 'there is a remarkable variety of draught and bottled beers up and down the country' before bemoaning the conservatism of drinkers in sticking to only one or two. 'One rarely hears of gourmets,' notes Baillie, 'who do not like a variety of, for instance, cheeses; nor do wine connoisseurs limit their tippling to a favourite château or vineyard.'

Yet when it comes to illustrating this apparent variety of flavour, Baillie leaves us none the wiser. His book distinguishes 'types' of beers and lists each brewery's beer, but has more to say about their pub liveries than what their products actually taste like. 'Some draught beers', we read, 'are distinctly "malty", and others "nutty". Some are extremely sweet and lack the *characteristic taste of beer*" (my italics). A few beers, mainly Bitters, merit the briefest of tasting notes – Arkell's has 'a pleasant nutty flavour', Brains and Everards are 'well-balanced', Hook Norton offers a 'draught bitter with the smack of hops' while Theakston Old Peculier is merely 'of distinctive flavour'. Many milds are simply listed as 'a darkish mild' or 'a light mild'.

Another influential text of the early British beer consumer movement, Richard Boston's *Beer and Skittles* (1976), proclaims with misinformed patriotism that 'In this country we have a greater variety of beer than anywhere else in the world'. But aside from railing against blandness and standardisation and making a few basic distinctions of bitter, sweet and malty, Boston fails to demonstrate quite what this variety consists of.

By now the *Good Beer Guide* had added its own brief notes in the now familiar Breweries section. In the 1977 edition, Brakspear Special is 'rich and slightly sweet', Palmers Best Bitter is 'thin and pleasant', and Old Peculier is 'rich and heavy'. Hydes light mild is 'light and hoppy' while the same brewery's dark mild is – you've guessed it – 'dark and hoppy'. Numerous beers are labelled 'distinctive', among them Adnams Bitter, Bateman XB, Belhaven 80/- and Taylor Landlord, but quite what distinguishes them is not explained.

To the modern beer aficionado, this apparent gap in the narrative seems curious. Sensory experience may not be the only factor in the appreciation of beer, but it is surely a major one. It's tempting to attribute the sparseness of description to

British cultural reserve about sensuality but, while I'm sure that played a part, the use of relative terms such as 'distinctive' and the recourse to tautologies like 'beery' points to something more obvious: that the basic taste of beer was taken for granted.

This is not surprising since, despite what Baillie and Boston say, the spectrum of flavours on offer in Britain was already severely squeezed. Beer historian Ronald Pattinson says that at the beginning of the 20th century, 'you could walk into a pub and have a choice of five or six draught beers such as Bitter, Mild, Burton and Porter, all completely different in character and with strengths ranging from 3% to 7 or 8% ABV'. By the early 1970s several of these historic styles had vanished and session-strength Bitter had achieved a commanding ubiquity. It's indicative that the first few issues of the *Good Beer Guide* categorise beers by using only three symbols — for Bitter, Mild and 'old ale or special'.

But the horizons of beer appreciation were soon to become dramatically widened. CAMRA began as a preservation movement, but opened up opportunities for new micro-breweries keen on innovation. Interest grew in beers that stretched the everyday repertoire, including revivals of historic styles, seen most dramatically in the resurrection of porter in 1978. Porter expanded the repertoire of stronger, darker tastes, which for most British drinkers had formerly been represented only by Guinness. It certainly raised the need for new adjectives: Roger Protz told me that his 'pretentious' language was first challenged when he described a porter as 'chocolaty'.

The discovery of world beer styles was arguably an even greater factor in highlighting the poverty of our vocabulary. The trailblazer here was Michael Jackson, whose pioneering *World Guide to Beer* (1977) is surprisingly sparse on tasting notes, though its richly detailed accounts of beer history and culture across the world were mouth-watering enough to inspire a generation of beer travellers. Imagine a British drinker in the late 1970s, reared on 'well balanced', 'pleasantly nutty' and 'beery' cask ale, confronted in Belgium with, say, a traditional gueuze, a Rodenbach Grand Cru and an Orval, and grappling with a way to communicate the experience.

As cask beer returned to British pubs, it became clear that cask conditioning did not of itself guarantee an interesting pint. Following motions at CAMRA's 1983 Annual General Meeting condemning increasing blandness and mediocrity, the 1984 *Guide* editorialises on the importance of being 'able to talk intelligently about the taste of beer. If the customer wants to persuade breweries to produce a beer he likes, he has to be able to say what they should taste like'. It goes on to argue for a common vocabulary of beer tasting.

Indeed by then such a vocabulary existed within the brewing industry: the 'Beer Flavor Wheel', developed in the early 1970s by brewing scientist Dr Morten Meilgaard at the Stroh brewery in Detroit, Michigan. This encompasses 44 different flavour components grouped into 14 categories, covering aroma, taste, mouthfeel and unintentional 'off' flavours. The wheel was meant as a tool for trained tasting panels, helping ensure consistency and pin-pointing technical issues. It was never intended to aid appreciation by the drinker, but nonetheless its vocabulary has seeped into the domain of consumer beer writing. This ranges from easily recognisable everyday terms – 'nutty', 'grassy', 'floral', 'hoppy', 'fruity' – through more surprising but evocative taste metaphors such as 'leathery', 'resinous' and 'medicinal' to the sort of terminology that was once reserved for the brewery laboratory, like 'diacetyl' (a buttery note) or 'acetaldehyde' (an off flavour like bruised apple).

As Cyril Pearl's character Acton had already discovered, the world of wine, where the tasting note was common currency, also offered a potential model. During the 1980s the image of fine wine was changing from an expensive and exclusive drink to one that offered affordable and accessible sophistication. A leading champion of wine's new image was the BBC's *Food and Drink* programme, first broadcast in 1982, in which presenter Jilly Goolden, often in the company of Oz Clarke, trampled on convention with a succession of apparently spontaneous and subjective taste associations. Clarke, also a keen beer drinker, told me that he and Goolden deliberately set out to democratise wine appreciation, asserting the validity of the ordinary drinker's immediate taste impressions alongside those of the trained taster or critic. Their flamboyant and sometimes outlandish comparisons were frequently parodied and ridiculed, but they certainly didn't do wine sales any harm.

The problem of how to 'talk intelligently about the taste of beer' continued to defeat CAMRA for a few more years, and the change, when it finally came, was a dramatic one. In 1989 the organisation set up members' tasting panels. Their collective opinion first appeared in the 1990 *Good Beer Guide*, where, alongside several pages on beer styles and flavours and pieces by Jackson and Clarke, it gushes with all the energy of an overconditioned Real Ale in a Bottle finally released from beneath its crown cap.

Marston's Pedigree is 'golden brown with a fruity aroma; a clean, well-hopped flavour, and fruity, nutty finish, slowly giving way to bitterness.' Robinson's Old Tom is 'dark brown, powerfully malty-fruity smelling, with a texture reminiscent of port [and an] intense fruity flavour, yet with a dry (though occasionally rather harsh) finish.' The sometimes sulphurous aroma of Shepherd Neame Master Brew is 'like a wet dog'. Old Peculier is merely 'Notorious, rich and heavy,' though by the following year its praises are sung in an entire evocative paragraph: 'Not quite as black as sin, as a delicate copper-red shows through, but its impressive colour prepares the drinker for an outburst of malt and fruit on the nose. The flavours are complex, but roast malt and butterscotch stand out, with a gently, hoppy bitterness and even forest fruit notes. The aftertaste is lasting and reveals that hops play a major part in the making of this rich, full-bodied beer.'

Some CAMRA members were not amused. A few months into the job, new *Good Beer Guide* editor Jeff Evans found himself having to defend the very existence of tasting notes at the 1990 AGM. *What's Brewing* reported: 'Flowery language and the wine bar image…was rejected in a motion from South Herts branch. Simon Holt said the Campaign should keep the findings of its tasting panels to itself and not publicise them in WH Smith's. He said many of the descriptions were the hallmark of Southern middle-class beer snobs. "We'll be laughed out of the public bar," he added.'

Evans recalls that while he agreed to rein back some of the wilder comparisons, he made a robust case for the tasting notes overall. 'I argued that as a Campaign of people who appreciate and advocate beers with a wide variety of flavours, we surely couldn't be satisfied with descriptions like "dark and smooth" and "distinctive",' he told me. His arguments won the day and the notes stayed, though they've become notably more prosaic over the years, a tendency partly explained by issues of space as the number of new breweries and new beers expanded. The notorious Old Peculier is now 'slightly malty but with hints of roast coffee and liquorice. A smooth caramel overlay and a complex fruitiness leads to a bitter chocolate finish.'

Meanwhile, beer writers found less restricted outlets for their detailed impressions of individual beers, as the tasting note became the stock in trade of the growing shelves of beer books. The first edition of Jackson's hymn to *The Great Beers of Belgium*, oozing apricot-tinged lambics and red ales 'with suggestions of Madeira, passion-fruit, oakiness and hints of iron', appeared in 1991, alongside Protz's *Almanac* and Tim Webb's first Belgian guide. Today there's a whole genre of books built around notes for canonical lists of 'must try before you die' beers.

By the time Evans was liberated from the strictures of the tasting panels with the first edition of his *Good Bottled Beer Guide* in 1997, a new medium was beginning genuinely to democratise the language and practice of tasting. The internet has made it possible for anyone to record their sensory impressions of a beer and share it with the world in seconds – ratebeer.com, for example, has around three million reviews of 130,000 different beers. While not all online tasting notes are well written or attractive, the internet has undoubtedly given a platform to many voices keen to champion and widen the appreciation of beer, including through intelligent responses to its flavours.

However many of the tensions remain. On the one hand there's the need to reflect variety and imagination and the personal, subjective response. On the other, there's the question of how informative a tasting note can really be without some form of shared framework. The industry has been slow to embrace taste descriptions. Copy on bottle labels usually contents itself with pretty stories and guff of the 'made from the finest malt and selected hops' variety. Retailers almost never extend the textual privileges of their wine lists to their beer offer, and the few that do are remarkable exceptions.

The Cyclops system, supported by CAMRA and now used by 214 breweries, has offered itself as an industry standard. But it seems to me unnecessarily reductionist, limited to no more than three words each for appearance, smell and taste plus ratings out of five for sweetness and bitterness. 'For too long,' state its promoters, 'we have used long, flamboyant tasting notes,' betraying some of the same fear of being laughed out of the public bar as the dissenters at CAMRA's 1991 AGM. Its insistence on terms 'aimed at the average drinker' points back to the tautological 1970s and a minimalism predicated on the assumption that most beers taste pretty similar, rather than raising drinkers' horizons.

In the United States, the celebration of beer is less encumbered by tradition and snobbery, inverted or otherwise. Here, some of the most intelligent responses to the problem of tasting have emerged partly thanks to the popularity of beer competitions, approaching the issue with seriousness without losing sight of pleasure and fun. A key text, Randy Mosher's marvellous *Tasting Beer* (2009), goes into as much detail as most of us could possibly want on flavour chemisty and beer styles, but concludes with an exhortation to total immersion in sensory enjoyment. 'Raise the glass, pause for a sniff, and then drink deep,' advises Mosher. 'Use your head, your heart, and your soul, and you can taste the whole world in it.' The world of beer that tastes beery is suddenly a long way away.

The author wishes to thank Iain Loe, Research and Information Manager at CAMRA, for his invaluable assistance.

DES DE MOOR is a beer writer and beer taster.
He writes regularly for *What's Brewing* and *Beer* and
is the author of *London's Best Beer, Pubs & Bars*.

Michael Hardman

Time to talk to pubgoers

MOST people who care about beer assume that most of the blame for the evils that have plagued British drinkers over the years lies with the Big Six national brewing companies that dominated the market in the second half of the 20th century. We have, however, largely ignored a sector that is equally as culpable as our traditional foes — the great, uninformed British public.

Look at that chap next to you. He's just asked for five pints of Carling and when the helpful lady behind the bar tells him the Carling's been taken off for good and replaced by Carlsberg, he looks as though he's been clonked on the head by a half brick. 'We don't like that Danish crap,' he complains. 'We're used to proper Canadian beer.' This over-confident connoisseur ignores the fact that Carling Black Label might be brewed in such typically Canadian places as Alton in Hampshire or that *probably the best lager in the world*, which he is now being offered, may well be brewed by Danes for Danes, but is produced at Carlsberg's plant in Northampton for the poor British drinker.

It wouldn't be polite though to intrude and put the fellow right, would it? No, we CAMRA chappies prefer a smug smile and an inward feeling of superiority over these folk who have swallowed gallons of television advertising. We'll tell our real-ale buddies about the incident at the next branch meeting and we'll all have a good laugh. But we won't do anything about it. Well, we should and we must, or else we might lose our cherished pint forever.

We ought to have been alerted to this problem from the beginning, as one example among many illustrates. In the mid-1970s, the Newbury branch of CAMRA provided a ground-breaking beer festival in a marquee at the Berkshire County Show, with dozens of real ales on display. One of the first customers was a man who ordered a pint of bitter, without being more specific than that. 'Which one would you like?' he was asked. 'Oh!' he replied. 'I'm not fussy. Watney's will do.'

Three and a half decades later, nothing seems to have changed, except that mass-produced keg beer has been replaced by mass-produced lager wrapped up in fake foreignness, and the share of the overall British beer market enjoyed by cask-conditioned beer has shrunk from perhaps 40 per cent to somewhere between 12 and 15 per cent, depending on whose figures you believe. Not every beer lover lies awake at night worrying about real ale's market share, surrounded as we are by 5,500 or so beer brands from 840 breweries compared with probably no more than 1,000 from 92 brewing companies at CAMRA's inception in 1971.

Most of us are delighted that so many new breweries have sprung up and we are revelling in the choice in many of our locals. But we should glance over our shoulders at the activities of the four global conglomerates that have replaced the dreaded Big Six of the 1970s and are now brewing eight out of ten pints produced in Britain. Only a trace of that output is cask beer, a style that none of the four seems to understand. It is an inconvenience to them.

There is no more room for complacency today than when we launched what people called our hopeless cause all those years ago. It is in every discerning drinker's interest that the industry supplying our needs is in robust health. We need more people drinking real ale to secure its future – many more than CAMRA's impressive membership of 130,000.

Cask-conditioned beer relies on quick sales. If it lies around in the pub cellar for more than a few days, it goes off. It either has to be poured down the drain, which eats into the pub's profit, or served up in foul condition, which puts people off drinking it and sends them along the bar to the lager and Guinness fonts. Unfortunately, far too many beers are still being served a long way off their peak condition. We have been telling pub companies and publicans for years that they will never do justice to our living, natural beers if they have too many of them on the bar. We must continue to persuade them to limit their range to match their sales so that what comes out of their pumps is wholesome and enjoyable.

Judging by the drastic drop in the consumption of cask beer, there are now only a quarter of the people drinking it compared with 40 years ago, or perhaps the same number of people each drinking a quarter of the amount of ale they used to do before the Health Police and the Band of Do-Gooders went to work in earnest, brandishing propaganda about a safe number of units that was plucked out of thin air without any scientific backing.

CAMRA's main forays into educating the public have been the publication of the annual *Good Beer Guide*, the Great British Beer Festival and the local counterparts of both, which have exceeded all the expectations of the early campaigners but still reach only a tiny proportion of the overall drinking population. We now need a concerted campaign to convert diehard lager drinkers to good old British traditional beer. We need to invest some of CAMRA's funds into devising a programme of education to dispel the myths and prejudices that surround both ale and lager. And we should consider persuading brewers to band together to buy television advertising to promote cask ale generically in the way that milk and egg producers have successfully done in the past.

If CAMRA's leaders, and ordinary members too, give some attention to this proposal, many more plans of action will surely surface. But perhaps we could start by buying a lager-drinking friend or colleague a pint of real ale. It would be a small price to pay in the fight for the future of the unique British product that we love.

MICHAEL HARDMAN MBE is one of the founding members of CAMRA. He edited the *Good Beer Guide* and *What's Brewing* and was for many years the public relations consultant to Young's Brewery in Wandsworth, south London. He was awarded the MBE in 2009 for his services to the brewing industry and CAMRA.

The beer revival

Stuart Bateman

Keeping it in the family

BATEMAN's: 137 years of brewing beer, selling beer and running pubs – sounds great doesn't it? It is – but that doesn't mean there isn't a lot of hard work, dedication, thought and endeavour involved, and the occasional frustration and failure. But I wouldn't change it for the world, even at a time when industry, especially small businesses, are facing some daunting challenges.

It has not been an easy 137 years, but much of the reason for our continued success is down to us following the ethos of my and my sister Jackie's grandfather, who said in 1954: 'Always treat your staff and tenants as you would wish to be treated yourself.'

That, and a lot of determination and occasional pig-headedness. But when you're hell-bent on retaining independence, stubbornness can be a good quality.

After the Beer Orders of the late 1980s, many brewers broke up their businesses and specialised in certain areas. On the whole they either focused on brewing or pubs.

We decided to specialise in all areas. Being a vertically integrated business makes it quite complicated, but it means there is always so much variety and we have a greater chance of meeting the needs of the retailer and consumer, as everything is in our own control. We are brewers, packagers, distributors, wholesalers, retailers, franchisers, property owners, machine operators and wine and spirit merchants. Complicated it might be, but when it gets in your blood then the challenge and excitement just makes you want to be successful and keep going.

Our success has been built on the fact that our shareholders and directors have all bought into the same vision and accept what the strategy, risks and rewards will be. This has been helped by the fact that many of our shares have been put into trust, which was an agreement my sister and I had with our parents. This was possible as we both agreed on how the company should move forward and what the ultimate goals would be – retaining independence being the main one.

I do not envy family businesses that have many family shareholders, some of whom do not work for the business, have not bought into the philosophy and are not receiving a realistic dividend. Being small we have to utilise all of our strengths. When competing for supply contracts, if we wanted to go head-to-head with bigger companies on the basis of who has got the biggest cheque book, or who is prepared to work on the smaller margins, then there is only going to be one winner. Take them on with speed of reaction, flexibility, imagination, endeavour and attention to detail and we've demonstrated we have more than a fighting chance.

We can be flexible because we don't have endless tiers of management and company regulations or rigid procedures and – most important – our beer is brewed by brewers, not accountants who have had every possible penny taken out of the production costs. Having a tight management structure also means we can be innovative and speedy with our new product development. We will try something and if it doesn't work we just move on to something else. We have had quite a few failures, but we brush ourselves down and move on, be it with flavoured beers, tenancy agreements, dual action beer sparklers, bottle presentation or 3D pump clips. Having said that, our clove beer tasted like mouthwash!

It has not always been a bed of roses. Our family divided in the late 1980s, which resulted in my aunt and uncle leaving the company and as a result the brewery was starved of investment for quite a few years while loans had to be repaid. The only way forward, without capital available, was to roll up our sleeves and develop our free trade, which Carlsberg subsequently purchased, paying more for it than we had had to borrow to meet the requirements of my aunt and uncle. We are now back in the free trade and have built it up to a similar size as it was prior to Carlsberg's acquisition, but this time the profits are being ploughed back into the business rather than used to pay off loans.

It was a great honour to be judged Pub Company of the Year (2009) and then Regional Brewer of the Year (2010) by *Publican* magazine, which was partly due to the innovative work we have done with our code of practice and the ground-breaking way we handle tenancies. Many have asked how we managed to complete our code of practice so quickly and produce a document many have copied. It was easy really, as there was nothing in it which we were not already doing. We merely formalised everything into one easy-to-read document.

As well as being the first with our code of practice, we have had other firsts with our tenancy agreements. We have done away with what we see as the archaic practice of the inventory purchase arrangement being the main means of entry into taking a pub tenancy, as there is little or no correlation between potential profitability and the level of ingoing cost. We have set the ingoing costs according to the potential profit that a tenant can make. For too long pub companies have taken on prospective tenants who have the most finance available, rather than being the most suitable to run a pub business. This has had serious consequences for the industry.

Other developments include agreements that pay tenants for increasing the value of the goodwill and reward them for investing in their own pubs. We have also introduced transparency into the 'wet rent' calculation, whereby tenants pay more for their products in return for paying less than a market rent. The result is that we are among the breweries that have the fewest pub vacancies in the industry.

We have been able to achieve this partly because we are small, flexible and forward-thinking and are able to look at the long term and build our balance sheet in order to help preserve independence, rather than looking for short-term profit, which can often be at the expense of individuals and the long-term health of a company.

With regard to possible future government and EU intervention, especially relating to the brewery tie, companies of our size could hide behind 'deminimus', whereby the regulations would not apply to us due to our size. But this would be very short sighted. We have to be in the situation where we are able to compete with and beat the offers of the big pub companies, and that means continuing to use our strengths and be forward thinking, in order to remain attractive to potential tenants.

But whatever the future brings we will tackle it head on and remember – pubs, people and beer: it doesn't get much better than that!

STUART BATEMAN is managing director of George Bateman & Son of Wainfleet, Lincolnshire.

Susan Nowak

For forty years CAMRA has had a fundamental impact on real ale – and for the last twenty on pub food too. In the late eighties, when 'pub grub' was the butt of stand up comedians and often leapt fully formed from a microwave oven, CAMRA was the first to publish a guidebook dedicated to pub food.

Good Pub Food put pubs serving real food as well as real ale on the map. It highlighted tasty, good value home-made meals including (long before we'd heard of food miles) pubs using local produce to cook regional recipes. It gave respect to classic pub dishes like steak and ale pie...and a platform to talented young chefs who chose to work in pubs instead of restaurants.

Today CAMRA's campaigning members continue to highlight excellent food as well as fine ale – though the pub food scene has expanded and changed beyond recognition. We face the challenge of gastropubs – showcases for food with flair and a bar with handpumps of well kept ale at their best – but too often pretentious quasi-restaurants with pricey wine lists.

CAMRA must do all it can to prevent decent pubs with modest menus being closed by greedy operators to reopen as guzzling gastropubs where locals no longer find a space at the bar.

In the UK our drinking heritage is ale not wine, so let's get it on the dining table. Encourage publicans to match beer to food, produce beer tasting notes, talk to diners about different beer styles and how they complement different dishes, serve it in attractive glasses – and from big bottles for sharing; use it to cook delicious dishes. Let's put beer at the heart of our eating out culture just as it is in our great brewing neighbours such as Belgium and Germany.

SUSAN NOWAK is a prolific writer on beer and food and contributor to CAMRA's *What's Brewing* and *Beer*.

Julian Grocock

Small brewers:
history with a future

HISTORY isn't what it used to be, so they tell me. Not a buzzing subject, at least, in 21st-century classrooms that echo to the thrills of Media Studies, Graphic Design, Fashion Photography and something called Citizenship, which today's little darlings have to be taught, apparently. Not one of my three daughters has taken History to GCSE level. It's not a core curriculum subject any more. Apparently.

Well, to this proud owner of a History 'Desmond', that's a disgrace. And in anticipation of a crescendo of accusations – that since I gave up teaching 28 years ago I have failed to put my degree to its academic use – I will quietly point out that the Almighty obviously has a Plan. Because here is an opportunity to demonstrate the true value of an educated historical perspective, specifically with reference to a life and career dedicated to beer, pubs and brewing.

So, in order to look forward, please allow me to take you back a little...

In 1977 Newark-on-Trent was an uncharacteristically exciting place. Nothing much of note had happened there since my birth 23 years before (and I doubt many flags flew

on that inauspicious occasion) but on 10 August the
Nottinghamshire market town became the slightly
bewildered beneficiary of the arrival of something called a
'real ale pub'. In those days, the Old King's Arms, opened by
former CAMRA chairman Chris Holmes, was a true pioneer –
a free house offering an astounding choice of *five* cask beers,
including such legends as Ruddle's County, Sam Smith's
Old Brewery Bitter and Marston's Pedigree.

And not long after the pub started trading the
excitement was heightened still further by the appearance
on the bar of an unfamiliar beer. It was called Regal Bitter,
came from Westcrown, a new brewery on George Street,
and was the only real ale indigenous to a once-renowned
brewing town now monopolised by the Courage/John Smith's
megalithic corporation. Local brewing heritage was
represented solely by the former James Hole's plant,
which a few years before had been emasculated to produce
nothing but keg and bright beers.

Like the Old King's Arms, Westcrown was a pioneer –
an early example of what would come to be known as a
micro-brewery. It was among the first ten or so to be opened,
along with the likes of tiny heroes such as Traquair, Selby,
Pollards, Litchborough, Blackawton, Godson, Penrhos
and Smiles. Of course in those days, even more than now,
the established industry had routes to market stitched up,
with a rigidly foreclosed tied estate system that meant,
in Newark for example, one Watneys pub, four belonging
to Home Brewery, and more than 30 Courage houses.
Only the Old King's Arms and one other place were free of tie;
and apart from the 'King's' I cannot recall another permanent
listing for Regal Bitter anywhere.

The Brewers' Society ran itself like an old boys' club, viewed these 'amateur' interlopers with disdain and deemed them too small for membership. Thus SIBA was born. Founded as the Small Independent Brewers' Association on 26 January, 1980, at a meeting of twenty micro-brewers in the Cross Keys at Wootton Bassett in Wiltshire, the subsequent history of the organisation, including its name change in 1995 to the Society of Independent Brewers, has been well documented – at least up to 2005 when a booklet was produced to mark its 25th anniversary.[1]

I can claim no connection with SIBA in those early days, except for the fact that a member of the inaugural committee was Norman Rutherford, who owned Westcrown with his brother Alan, and I drank their beer. As it happens, the brewery was sold and renamed Priory later in 1980, and sadly closed in 1983. Such has been the fate of a host of micros over the years. Survivors from the early days are few: Traquair still brews, and others that have been around for thirty years or more include Ballard's, Blackawton (originally in Devon – now in Cornwall), Broughton, Butcombe, Chiltern, Cotleigh, Exmoor, Goose Eye, Moorhouse's, Ringwood (now owned by Marston's), Wood's and Woodforde's. There have been numerous changes of ownership and geographical relocations so it is difficult to compile a definitive and comprehensive list.

However, the brewing revolution that followed in the wake of the trailblazers is no secret. My first *Good Beer Guide* (1976) listed 154 breweries (owned by just 85 companies); thirty-five years later there are 840 and still counting. The idealistic inspiration, for redundant 'rationalised' professionals and home-brewing enthusiasts alike, was fuelled at first by the

---

1. *A History of The Society of Independent Brewers 1980–2005* by Nicholas Redman

unprecedented success of a consumer-led campaign to persuade an industry to change direction. CAMRA hit on the mood of the moment, but that historical perspective thing has proved it to be much more than that. Forty years and still going stronger than ever is a pretty long moment.

In addition to the unity of purpose of a popular movement, don't underestimate the importance to the brewing renaissance of the cussed independence and individualism of those prepared to sink themselves, their families and their fortunes so totally into the lifestyle-defining and all-consuming commitment required to run a small brewery business. Economic stability was extremely difficult to achieve – as proved by the many that went to the wall – and for most dreams of actually accruing wealth remained just that.

All too often, neither dedication to the good beer cause nor single-mindedness of business spirit was enough to keep fledgling breweries afloat. Even together they could fall short. While some youthful enterprises have indeed stood the recurring tests of time to reach a level of maturity, too many others, just as driven and just as dogged – and brewing beer that was just as delicious – have failed nonetheless. So when we consider the factors that have contributed to a vibrant modern industry that promises so much for the future, there is an absolutely crucial one that must be taken into account.

Almost from its inception SIBA fought for duty concessions for micro-brewers to offset the diseconomies of their small-scale production. These were already in place in other EEC brewing nations, but it took more than twenty years of persistent argument and a refusal to go away and lie down quietly before the lumbering wheels of Whitehall finally responded and rolled out their own legislation.

On 17 April 2002, Chancellor Gordon Brown made his historic Budget announcement that Small Brewers' Relief (or Progressive Beer Duty) would at last be introduced. This meant that the first 59 barrels brewed each week by small brewers would be charged at half the standard rate of duty.

This is history with a future. The immediate effect was to save several small brewers from likely collapse and give them a lifeline to build viable long-term businesses. Subsequently, and as a direct result of the availability of duty relief, micro-brewing entered a period of sustained expansion and volume growth. According to its industry survey conducted in late 2010, at least half of SIBA's 470 members began brewing after 2002. And if they were jumping on a bandwagon – or indeed a brewer's dray – it has been entirely to the benefit of beer drinkers.

In the 2012 *Good Beer Guide*'s index of permanent brands nearly 5,500 real ales are listed, to which can be added at least 1,500 seasonals, specials and one-offs. A quick count in the breweries section of that first Guide I bought thirty-five years ago – a ridiculously easy task – reveals just 300 draught beers. Some of these were the same brands from different breweries – six were called Whitbread Trophy. Furthermore, more than 90 per cent were bitters and milds, whereas today's portfolio also embraces golden ales, stouts, porters, IPAs, old ales, barley wines, wheat beers, fruit and other speciality beers, and cask lagers. For those of us old enough to see five hand-pumps on a bar and feel like lounge lizards let loose in a harem, this promiscuity of choice is nothing short of fan-bloody-tastic.

A cautionary note though: just as CAMRA continues to fight for consumers, SIBA cannot relax its efforts on behalf of brewers, because history teaches us that being where we are now does not guarantee where we will be tomorrow. Persistently rising duty threatens untold harm to beer and pubs, in a country whose beer tax revenue already makes up 40% of the total raked in by twenty-seven EU member states. It may be true that PBD sugars the pill for those who receive it, but duty hikes intensify calls from larger non-qualifying brewers for its drastic revision, or even its abolition. Having contributed so much, it is frightening to imagine the devastation that would be precipitated by the withdrawal of relief, and its defence is of paramount importance.

Pubs remain at the heart of what we do. SIBA has achieved much through its Direct Delivery Scheme into the tied estates of giant pubcos, but the tied system needs to develop further towards optional trading freedoms. Government too must join up its thinking to protect the beleaguered pub hospitality sector; and harm-reduction campaigners should recognise the role played by well run and well populated community pubs in fostering a responsible drinking culture.

But the concluding message has to be positive. The real beauty of British brewing today lies in its unique evolution of past into present, whereby the history and heritage of an ancient craft have blended with the innovation and imagination of a youthful modern industry, to create an environment for enterprise in which sustainable localised production, choice, diversity and quality increasingly take precedence over the macro-economic thinking that hitherto led inexorably to centralisation, monopolisation, rationalisation, bland big brand dominance and reduction of choice.

Chris Holmes is still at the helm of the business that opened the Old King's Arms – now based around the esteemed and successful Castle Rock Brewery – and I've read recently that Alan Rutherford and his sons are reviving the Westcrown name, hopefully with a new brewery at their Derbyshire pub.

It's as refreshing as a pint – of Regal Bitter then or Harvest Pale now – to note that the direction taken by this most people-focused world of beer and pubs has for forty years now been decided by the people who have dedicated themselves to it.

JULIAN GROCOCK is Chief Executive of the Society of Independent Brewers.

Mike Selvey

I first came across CAMRA at Birmingham's Bingley Hall in 1983. We were in the middle of a county championship match at Edgbaston and the day was a washout. So at 11 o'clock, we all decamped to the Great British Beer Festival where we gave it our best shot but spent rather too long. Twelve hours in fact. However, it did serve to reinforce how much life there was still in the great tradition of British brewing despite the best efforts of the big companies to kill it off with the ghastly keg stuff. Red Barrel, Whitbread Trophy. Makes me shudder just to think of the names and see the displays on the pumps. CAMRA was to become the most successful of all consumer campaigns, the fruits of which we see today with the stunning rise in the numbers of micro-breweries and the relative decline in consumption of what the landlord of one of my locals calls Eurofizz. They are still with it with their gassy John Smith's Smooth and the likes. But they will not win. It is simple really. Just a matter of taste.

MIKE SELVEY was a seam bowler who played for England, Middlesex, Surrey and Glamorgan. He is now the cricket correspondent of the *Guardian*.

Jeff Evans

How beer got its bottle back

MUCH has been made – quite rightly – of the resurgence of cask-conditioned beer during CAMRA's first 40 years. Less has been said about the way bottled beer, and in particular bottle-conditioned beer, has similarly bounced back but, in many ways, it's an even more remarkable tale. It is believed that, when CAMRA was founded in 1971, just five bottle-conditioned beers – beers that included a natural yeast sediment for a secondary fermentation in the bottle – still existed. These beers were Worthington's White Shield, Guinness Extra Stout, Courage Imperial Russian Stout, Gale's Prize Old Ale and Eldridge Pope Thomas Hardy's Ale. They were revered for the fuller, fresher, more complex flavours the living yeast provided and they stood out because British bottled beer as a whole had become emasculated.

The decline had begun with Louis Pasteur's 19th-century experiments with heat treatment to control infection in beer. Soon pasteurisation became the norm at most breweries. Beers were filtered to remove yeast and then blasted with heat to kill off any yeast cells that survived. Dead, inert beer, artificially carbonated to give it some sparkle, became the norm in the bottled beer world years before it took over the draught beer environment.

With the famous five bottle-conditioned beers just about holding on to existence, the situation changed little during CAMRA's formative years, summed up by the experience of one Somerset brewery, the Miner's Arms at Priddy, which opened to produce only bottle-conditioned beer, but was a tiny, short-lived enterprise. As we moved into the 1980s, some adventurous small brewers – such as Burton Bridge in Staffordshire – began bottling on a limited scale, but the barometer of bottled beer's fortune hardly moved. Certainly there was no evidence of bottle-conditioned beer making a comeback on a national level. Even pasteurised bottled beer was in decline, with supermarkets and off-licence chains stocking no more than a very limited, bland selection of amber liquids, and only pubs offering some sort of last refuge for obscure, seemingly forgotten styles of beer, such as sweet brown ale and barley wine.

The situation prompted an article in the 1987 *Good Beer Guide*. It was not an optimistic feature. In a study of the state of bottled beer in Britain, it declared that 'By the end of the century, Britain's remaining breweries will produce between them no more than a dozen bottled beers'. Thankfully, on that occasion, the *Good Beer Guide* got it wrong. Within a few years, the bottled beer market was to open up dramatically.

As the number of small brewers continued to increase, so did the number of bottled beers they offered. True, these beers were very parochial and produced in minuscule quantities, but they were useful to brewers finding it difficult to secure sales of cask beer to pubs. Using elementary, hand-operated equipment, they found they could use up those spare casks of unsold ale and sell bottled beer to the local off-licence or from their own brewery shop. And, because breweries of this size simply couldn't afford the equipment to filter and/or pasteurise the beers – not that most of them wanted to do that in any case – these beers were mostly bottle conditioned.

This trend was boosted with the introduction of the Beer Orders in 1989, which encouraged even more brewers to start up, hoping to grab some of the action in newly-freed-up national brewers' pubs. It didn't quite work out the way many of them hoped. Brewers – in cahoots with newly-formed pub companies – still managed to squeeze small brewers out of the market, so many of the newcomers turned to the bottle.

A government extension to the Guest Beer Law allowed tenants of national brewers' pubs to sell a bottle-conditioned beer of their own choosing, as well as a cask beer, but it's hard to suggest that this had much impact. Of more importance, it can be argued, was the influence of beer writers in opening drinkers' eyes to the variety that was now available and the fact that new outlets were being discovered by brewers. This was the time when specialist beer shops began to proliferate, when farm shops and craft centres were looking to widen their range of local products, when even supermarkets began to understand that their customers wanted diversity and a not restricted choice, be it in bread, cheese or beer. The arrival of the internet, to spread the word about great beer and even to offer an alternative means of beer retailing, similarly had a major bearing on the bottled beer scene.

Then, of course, there's the CAMRA input. Just how important this has been over the years is not clear, but the resurgence in bottle-conditioned beer production does tie in closely to decisions made by the Campaign. In 1991, a motion at the CAMRA AGM called for the organisation to do more to promote bottle-conditioned beer. From that time, the *Good Beer Guide* began to list such beers alongside cask ales and a new category was added to the Champion Beer of Britain awards, to recognise the best bottle-conditioned beers. But CAMRA was not finished there. In 1998, it published the first edition of the *Good Bottled Beer Guide*, a book entirely devoted to bottle-conditioned beer, or real ale in a bottle, as CAMRA began to call it. Over the years, the Guide has acted as a yardstick for the growth of the bottle-conditioned beer sector. From featuring just 170 beers in the first edition, the seventh edition, published in 2009, included details of more than 1,300 beers, and the numbers just keep on rising.

CAMRA's support for bottle-conditioned beer continues. Producers can now apply for a logo to add to their labels. This 'CAMRA says this is real ale' badge helps customers pick out naturally-conditioned beers from other bottled beers. There are also promotional materials available to retailers who want to support this now substantial sector.

Perhaps the best indication of how established bottle-conditioned beer has become in Britain is the way in which even big brewers have become part of the success story. Seeing how micro-brewers have opened up new markets by bottle conditioning beer, some of the country's major firms have now added their own equivalent products. Famous names such as Shepherd Neame, Wells & Young's, Adnams, Hook Norton, St Austell, Thwaites, Harveys, Samuel Smith, Marston's and Greene King all now have bottle-conditioned beers in their portfolios. Fuller's has gone a step further. Having joined the market early, in 1995, with its excellent 1845 ale, it has progressed to releasing a special Vintage Ale

each year and – echoing moves by many smaller brewers –
adding recreations of historic beer styles to its selection.
In 2010, the Past Masters series was introduced, with each
beer a reconstruction of a recipe discovered in the Fuller's
brewing books.

Fuller's is also today responsible for the production of
Prize Old Ale, one of the five bottle-conditioned beers still
standing in 1971. White Shield (now actively marketed by
current owner Molson Coors) is also still available and there
are hopes that Courage Imperial Russian Stout may soon be
re-introduced by Wells & Young's. Sadly we've lost Thomas
Hardy's Ale and Guinness Extra Stout, but, when we now
have upwards of 1,300 bottle-conditioned beers to choose
from, we can't be too despondent, can we?

JEFF EVANS writes the *Good Bottled Beer Guide* and
is a former editor of the *Good Beer Guide*.

External
influences

Julie Johnson

The view from across the pond

AS CAMRA celebrates its 40th anniversary, it enjoys a reputation as one of the most effective grass-roots organisations of the 20th century, with a membership of 130,000 and credit for having changed British beer culture. But only 330 of those members live in the United States – a mere one-quarter of one percent of the total. It would be tempting to conclude that CAMRA's influence stops at the Atlantic coast.

Most Americans have never heard of CAMRA, including many of the supporters of the American 'beer revolution' of the past three decades. Craft and speciality beer, the most vibrant and talked-about sector of American beer, represents only about five percent of the market, and real ale aficionados are a slim niche within that niche.

But CAMRA's impact has been profound. When Americans attend beer festivals, support beer education programmes and activism, experiment with real ale, host 'cask nights' at local beer bars, or express their passion for traditional brewing, they owe a debt to CAMRA – even when they don't know it, or when the form of that tribute sometimes falls outside activities that CAMRA itself would sanction.

Our two countries hit low points in their brewing histories in the second half of the last century. Both of these great beer-drinking nations faced impoverished beer scenes, but the underlying causes were different, as were the responses of their beer enthusiasts. Britain's endangered beer tradition gave rise to CAMRA; the United States went in another direction. As CAMRA supporters know well, Britain's national brewers turned their backs on traditional cask ale in the 1960s in favour of less perishable keg beer. In pubs, where the great majority of beer was consumed, handpumps for cask ale gave way to taps to dispense beer that was filtered and artificially carbonated.

American beer culture was very different. Despite our historic connections to Great Britain, our beer industry had been dominated since the 19th century by immigrants from Germany (even the proceedings of professional brewing societies here were long published in German). Brewing companies with names like Busch, Pabst or Schlitz produced pale lagers with German or Bohemian origins. Even before the turn of the century, American drinkers embraced progressively lighter-bodied beers than the European progenitors. In 1919, National Prohibition shuttered our breweries for 13 years. Afterwards, the shrunken roster of companies that re-opened grew shorter still with the consolidation of the industry into a few national brands. By 1980, only 40 breweries or so operated in the United States, almost all producing similar light lagers, destined largely for consumption at home.

British and American beer drinkers appear to have arrived at a similar point by the 1960s or 70s, which was a landscape of boring beer. But the similarities were superficial. British drinkers could see something they treasured, traditional cask ale, slipping away, and a rich pub culture with it. Faced with this threat, CAMRA emerged in 1971 as a preservationist organisation, a consumer-driven revolt against the changes wrought by big brewers. By contrast, for American beer drinkers, Budweiser and comparable beers had been established for nearly a century as the 'traditional' adult beverage of Americans. Frustrated beer lovers wanting more flavour turned to innovation, because there wasn't a tradition that needed saving. And the American beer revolution was led not by consumers but by a few eccentric entrepreneurs attempting to carve out new space in the shadow of the big brewers, not to change them.

Oddly enough, the most innovative first step American beer enthusiasts took was to rediscover the traditional British ale styles we had lost. CAMRA, to us, was the guardian of those styles. Home beer brewing was only legalised here in 1978, and appropriate technical information was hard to come by. Home brewers turned to CAMRA as a source of brewing expertise. In 1978, Charlie Papazian, a nuclear scientist and avid home brewer in Boulder, Colorado, founded the American Homebrewers Association. Three years later, he visited Britain for the first time to research the professional production of British ales. During that visit, he made a connection that is probably the most profound that links CAMRA with what followed in American craft brewing.

Papazian had met Michael Jackson in the US, and happened to visit Jackson when the Great British Beer Festival was taking place in Leeds. 'I guess Michael had mentioned to Roger [Protz] and the powers that be at the Great British Beer Festival that I was coming over, and that I was head of the then-American Homebrewers' Association,' he recalls. Papazian was invited to judge at the final best-of-show round — 'a pretty informal assessment of four or five beers on stage in front of everybody, with about four other blokes like myself who were evaluating the beer. We decided the champion beers right there on stage.'

But what struck Papazian was the GBBF itself. 'To go into this festival and see thousands — tens of thousands — of people coming over a period of four days, to me, it was a celebration of British beer. I really wasn't that deep into the politics of real ale versus other kinds of beer. I knew they were against certain types of beers — keg beers — but I didn't fully understand the dynamics. But they stood for something, and they stood for national pride in a tradition of beer.' Back in London, Papazian floated the idea of an American version of the festival. Jackson was supportive, but famously remarked, 'Well, that would be a great idea, Charlie, but where are you going to get the beer?'

The Great American Beer Festival debuted in 1982, a small gathering of American heritage breweries and three new micro-breweries. Today, the festival is the biggest and oldest in the United States and the model for hundreds of festivals across the country, and the associated competition is the nation's most prestigious. The GABF has nothing to do with real ale, and yet it owes everything to the spirit of CAMRA's GBBF.

Later, others would mount festivals explicitly to promote the appreciation of real ale in America. The first large effort was the Chicago Real Ale Festival, launched with the support of two beer writers and CAMRA members, Ray Daniels and Steve Hamburg. From 1996 to 2003, the festival grew to feature the largest number of British and American-brewed real ales, rigorously presented to CAMRA standards for an American audience. In 1997, NERAX, New England Real Ale Exhibition, opened in Somerville, Massachusetts, where it is now the oldest real ale event in the United States. The hosting organisation, CASC (the Cask-conditioned Ale Support Campaign), organises festivals in the American north-east, and works with 'brewers, publicans and the public to educate and promote cask ale by sharing technical information, pub crawls and other smaller events in which cask ale is served.' Through close co-operation with CAMRA, CASC brings British real ales to its events, and arranged for American real ales to be served at GBBF.

Though small, NERAX events regularly sell out, even though CASC president Mark Bowers admits, 'Most people in the US do not know of CAMRA, cask ale or real ale. However, most US brewers know of CAMRA, as well as real ale, whether they produce it or not. Most realise that CAMRA saved real ale back in the 70s and has been a powerful force in helping to keep real ale alive and well in the UK. Most lovers of real ale in the US owe a debt of gratitude to CAMRA for preserving cask ale, not just in the UK but for re-introducing it to the US with the rise of craft beer over the last 20 years or so.'

American craft brewers remain the most mindful of the debt the craft beer movement owes to CAMRA. A self-confessed fan of CAMRA since the 1990s, Matt Chappel devotes his brewery, Indigo Imp in Ohio, to cask and bottle-conditioned ales. 'As a home brewer I was always trying to brew authentic, traditional beers and thought that cask conditioning was the ultimate "Old School" method of producing and serving beer.'

Mad Fox Brewing Co. in Fairfax, Virginia is close enough to the nation's capital to attract employees of the British embassy to drink their cask ales. CEO and brewer Bill Madden is a member of CAMRA (one of the 330!) and supports his commitment to real ale with imported Angram hand pumps and two coolers at appropriate cellar temperature. His goal is to have 'three to four firkins in stillage waiting to be poured in proper condition (rather that doing the typical running out on a busy night's rush and rolling a fresh cask out to be tapped).'

Madden's careful attention to his casks stands in contrast to the real ales or cask ales presented by some American breweries or bars. Casks are set up in haste, and cloudy beers that an English drinker would be justified in sending back are accepted by customers who know no better. Worse, customers can be persuaded that a cloudy or poorly carbonated beer is part of the real ale experience.

Given the widespread public ignorance about cask ale, CAMRA publications have become valuable education tools for brewery representatives, bar managers and waiting staff. To have industry professionals rather than consumers setting standards for quality turns the original CAMRA model on its head, but it is the most effective way that CAMRA members based in the US educate drinkers in the relatively new experience of appreciating real ale.

Of course, one of the main influences of CAMRA on Americans has been as a reference to the best of British pubs. Tourists who pick up the *Good Beer Guide* may, again, be ignorant of both real ale and CAMRA, but the guidebook has steered many a naïve tourist into some of the country's best traditional pubs. They may arrive with the tedious American prejudice against 'warm, flat English beer,' but the pub experience may be the gateway to the beauty of proper real ale.

Forty years on, CAMRA members can be proud that the organisation has supported American beer culture in unexpected – if unseen – ways. CAMRA has helped educate us in beer quality and basic standards of service, it has helped nurture a respect for traditional beer styles and facilitated their return to the American scene, it has introduced cask ale to a small but devoted following, and it has made travel to Britain a richer experience through her beer and pubs. That's quite a contribution.

JULIE JOHNSON is the former editor of *All About Beer* magazine, published in Durham, North Carolina, and is now the magazine's Contributing Editor.

Zak Avery

World-wide choice

THERE can't be any doubt that beer culture in Britain has changed radically in the past 40 years. When CAMRA was founded, real ale was at its nadir, and now it is at its zenith. But what is surprising is that in parallel with the rise – or rebirth – of real ale, there has also been a boom in interest in other beers. While the beer market is indisputably in decline, there has never been a greater choice of beers in the pub, the supermarket, and the specialist off-licence.

While real ale may be Britain's signature gastronomic gift to the world, there is a world of other beer out there. I can't pretend to have seen this rise in its entirety over the past four decades – I'm only a year older than CAMRA – but I have seen how things have changed in the past 20 years. I've been lucky enough to speak to a few people who have watched both the rise of good quality imported beer and its gradual assimilation into the Great British Beer Festival.

The Bières Sans Frontières (BSF) bar at GBBF is a similar success story to that of cask ale. To visit it today, stuffed to the top of the scaffolding racks with rare beers and casked ales from unlikely countries, it's hard to believe that it started life as a 'foreign beer table'. Ian Garrett, who has had a long involvement with BSF recalls: 'In 1981 I worked at my first GBBF at Queens Hall in Leeds. It was there that the Foreign, that is Belgian, Beer Table was stuck down one side of the hall. There can't have been more than two dozen beers and I became immersed in the joys of Belgian beer'.

It's unsurprising that the first newcomers to the British import scene were Belgian beers. Belgium is geographically close and to those in the know it was, in beer terms, more diverse than Britain at the time (and still is, if truth be told). The international pariah – lager – had already established itself as tasteless, cold and fizzy, an image that it is only recently starting to shake off in Britain, and its increasing presence on the BSF bar surely signifies the start of a grassroots movement to embrace and promote 'real lager', whatever that may come to mean.

I was also unwittingly present at the early years of another brew that has come to be a gateway beer for many people – either commodity drinkers who have had their horizons broadened to embrace more flavoursome beer, or real ale stalwarts who, on trying it, are forced to concede that it defied expectations. In the early 1990s, I was an obnoxious twenty-something, living in Brooklyn, New York City, complaining loudly about the lack of good beer. Somebody put a newly-released Brooklyn Lager into my hand and that silenced my argument for good. If you still think that American beer is nothing to write home about, do yourself a favour and visit the BSF bar.

Another reason why this is the best time ever to be interested in good-quality beer is the sheer volume of importers, wholesalers and retailers in Britain. I've worked for Beer Paradise and its retail arm Beer-Ritz for the past

10 years. Other well-known importers include James Clay, Cave Direct, Vertical Drinks and a host of others responsible for bringing these beers to the drinking public. Further down the chain, great pubs and bars have caught the bug and brought an ever-widening selection of beer to an increasingly interested public. And crucially, the drinker is more receptive to these beers than ever before – it wouldn't work without the support of a legion of curious drinkers.

The other change in the last decade has been the rise of the internet. This has had a double-whammy effect on beer. Firstly, information about beer has become much more easily and cheaply accessible, and has undoubtedly contributed to the fetish for rare beer, and created a sense of the exotic around beers from far-flung countries. And secondly, the rise of mail-order beer websites has meant that, should you be sufficiently curious and have sufficient money, anything is within your grasp – quite a contrast to the not-so-distant days when drinking foreign beers meant travelling to foreign lands.

There is a lot of work involved getting a beer from a farmhouse brewery in Belgium, or the West Coast of the United State, into the glass of a drinker in Britain. None of it would be possible without the end consumer. While it's hard to demonstrate a cause and effect, it's no great leap of imagination to see the increased rise in real ale consumption and the rise in good quality 'world beer' (for want of a better term) as being linked. Personally, I don't mind whether they are both driven by the same people, or by different groups of people taking an interest in factors such as flavour, quality and provenance. For me, the simple fact is that if you love beer, this is a golden age.

ZAK AVERY is a beer retailer, taster and beer blogger. He was named Beer Writer of the Year in 2008 by the British Guild of Beer Writers.

Chris Bonington

Whenever I come home from a trip, one of the things I most look forward to is my visit to my local pub, the Old Crown in Hesket Newmarket, and a pint of my favourite brew – Doris's 90th. There is something so very special about the traditional English pub and well-kept and served ale. I believe that CAMRA has done a terrific job over the years in fostering and helping preserve this very important part of our heritage at a time when all too many pubs are either closing down or being turned into 'eateries' or giant and characterless drinking factories.

SIR CHRISTIAN BONINGTON CVO, CBE, DL, is a mountaineer who has made 19 expeditions to the Himalayas, including four to Everest. He made the first ascent of the south face of Annapurna. He is a shareholder in the co-operative that owns the Old Crown in Hesket Newmarket, Cumbria.

The challenge ahead

BILL TIDY, cartoonist and raconteur, has drawn the
Kegbuster strip in *What's Brewing* since the 1970s.

Alastair Gilmour

The danger of becoming a national treasure

IS it true that nobody loves a fairy when she's 40? The sentiment may be at the heart of an old music-hall ditty rather than the result of some socio-economic theory, but it could be the case. Apart from a robust membership of 130,803, do any of the remaining 62,131,197 population of this country really love CAMRA? What is the public impression of the organisation after 40 years?

Forty is old enough for mellow reflection, yet young enough to plan for a resurgent, revitalised future – it's also an opportunity to raise a few questions. Is it now time for CAMRA to settle back into self-congratulatory smugness or dust itself off and continue for another four decades? Doesn't a campaign lose its point after 40 years? Do 40-year-old aims and objectives disappear into wallpaper?

A campaign is a series of co-ordinated activities designed to achieve a social, political or commercial goal. Forty years is a long time to be campaigning and as the Campaign for Real Ale has existed since 1971, surely the goal has been scored and the match won?

A question then: is a name change overdue? SIBA, the organisation formed in 1980 to represent the interests of an emerging wave of micro-breweries, changed its name from the Small Independent Brewers' Association to the Society of Independent Brewers, but kept its acronym. It is regarded as a modern, fast-paced, flexible organisation.

Now let's compare CAMRA to the Thirty Year War, which started in 1618, primarily as a religious conflict in what is roughly now Germany. It ended in 1648 in a treaty called the Peace of Westphalia. I draw this comparison because for 62,131,197 souls, CAMRA is about as relevant to them as the Bourbon-Hapsburg rivalry at the core of the lengthy conflict.

When campaigns are launched they grab attention and gather momentum, they suck in supporters and repel sceptics as they roll on to their objective. And, crucially, there's usually a point where the campaign has been won, when all the effort has been justified and the world seems a better place. On the other hand, campaigns lose their thrust if they are stretched out; those who joined out of curiosity and novelty become bored with the same messages being repeated over and over and slope off to find another cause to follow, leaving the diehards and the zealots to wallow in self-righteousness.

The diehards and the zealots are then considered by outsiders – let's number them at 62,131,197 – to be extremists who have lost touch with reality, therefore their thoughts and opinions do not apply to the rest of society. But as long as they're not hurting anybody, the vast majority can ignore them and let them get on with their introspective lives.

That's the old stereotype, of course, and there's more. CAMRA members sport beards, wear sandals and dress exclusively in brewery polo-shirts (which they normally get free).

They eat lentils, are unkempt, have no sense of fashion or perambulatory co-ordination, they appear to collect carrier-bags and enjoy an arm's-length association with manners.

A Swiss brewer of organic beers I dined with a few years ago was interested in the concept of CAMRA as a national organisation. He hadn't fully appreciated that Britain had a significant group of volunteers who had his industry's interests at heart – until the franc dropped.

'Aah,' he said. 'Yes, of course, we have a similar thing here, too. They live with their mothers.'

Few of those stereotypes bear deep scrutiny, but they hang on and on because we all know one who conforms.

Outside looking in, CAMRA is in danger of becoming a national treasure, a Stephen Fry-equivalent where tolerance and indulgence are laid on thick to remind us that once upon a time here stood cutting edge – this was the alternative, but what we now see before us is an anachronism. National treasures are undoubtedly loved and cherished but exist to be patted on the head on occasion and given a niche role somewhere nice and safe and very, very sanitised. The world will continue to throw up challenges and spawn challengers but dear old national treasures will fail to notice that times have changed.

Enter keg. Every micro and its granny are experimenting with keg versions of their most popular ales. They have not all of a sudden abandoned their deep-rooted principles, but smell opportunity. The campaign, to them, has been won. Multi-national keg beer producers are finding life tough because fewer people want to drink what they process through their doors. They have flirted with their own cask-conditioned products and have taken over small breweries to give them another route to market that was previously denied them, which all suggests they may be feeling the pain and don't really know how to relieve it.

But opportunity knocks – outlets that normally wouldn't touch real ale with a cattle prod are in the sights of micros' keg (with taste and character) and they're lapping it up. David is approaching with his slingshot and while it'll take many, many throws to do terminal damage to Goliath, the intention is there and the sweat on the giant's brow is all too apparent.

But what does CAMRA think of this departure? Is there a policy to embrace well-produced, consistent, quality keg beer that's virtually indistinguishable from its 'live' cousin in a blind tasting? A seismic shift in policy is required to do that, but to ignore the phenomenon is to spiral into irrelevance. I hear much wailing and gnashing of membership cards.

There are surely posts on the CAMRA online forums that argue this point inside out, but there is nothing there to inform the casual visitor; it's as if the three-letter word must not be spoken. Beer tie reform, full measures, pub closures, social networking, cask ale week and ale trail promotion are highly laudable initiatives but fundamental moves like keg beer need more exposure, not apparent denial.

CAMRA therefore is at risk of taking on Mary Whitehouse's mantle – a cudgel-wielding force who stood up for her Christian beliefs and tried to hold back the tide of the 'permissive society' only to eventually become a figure of fun. (Billy Connolly: 'I wouldnae be happy either if my name rhymed with toilet.')

Similarly, the Prince of Wales – a man who probably means well but is stuck somewhere in a land of *Goon Show* scripts surrounded by Doric, Ionic and Corinthian columns – may champion beer-related causes, but as a figurehead he is not always taken seriously.

The media isn't kind to either beer or CAMRA – newspapers love phrases such as 'beer belly' and 'lager lout'. The words alliterate nicely and are convenient shortcuts into a reader's limited attention span. Inevitably, the story that follows a beer belly headline has nothing whatsoever to do with normal, law-abiding drinkers and pub-goers enjoying a convivial experience, but is more closely related to football hooliganism and racist behaviour.

My opinion is that the beer world is too diverse and complicated for the mainstream media to cope with. Journalists, apart from a few specialists, are bamboozled by the terminology – what's all this about managed houses, tied houses, tenancies and free houses? How can one sector of the beer industry report a 7 per cent decline and the 2011 *Good Beer Guide* say 99 more breweries had opened?

It's confusing. Faced with a beer story and a deadline, some journalists will squawk: 'Do I really have to swot up on the difference between Mild and Bitter before I can write this article with conviction and authority? Hang on, I'll just regurgitate this press release from GlobalBeerDotCom Plc, it's easier that way.' Believe me, it happens.

National food and drink magazines are no more interested in carrying beer stories than they are in underwater origami or dwile flonking. Cheese rolling gets more coverage than beer festivals and they'd rather give you the name of the world conker expert than reveal Champion Beer of Britain.

In a nation that sells 158 million Pot Noodles every year, it's a hard job for a freelance journalist to persuade a commissioning editor that a naturally-fermented product made from four ingredients can develop extraordinary aromas, flavours and aftertastes that can be – from sip one – a life-influencing experience.

While the beer industry as a whole is acknowledged to be in decline, there is plenty of evidence to suggest that real ale is striding along rather nicely, but we journalists rarely get the chance to write that there are people out there who want quality, variety and choice and not an instruction to 'Pour water up to the line, wait two minutes, stir and serve'. I once asked the editor of an award-winning food and drink publication if she would like some beer features. Her reply was: 'I don't like beer so it doesn't get in.' Her successor is from the same school of bitter denial. 'I have a problem with beer,' he emailed in response to my request (with attached samples) with no further expansion.

What do we do? Start up a campaign and go on a 40-year odyssey? Campaigns, as have been pointed out here, have a limited life, so isn't the Big Four-O an opportune moment for CAMRA to call itself something different? I've scoured the dictionary and all I can come up with are camisole, camp and camshaft, so let's go with Peace of Westphalia.

At least something that sounds cheesy will attract media attention.

ALASTAIR GILMOUR is a freelance journalist specialising in beer. He has been the British Guild of Beer Writers Beer Writer of the Year on four occasions and has been presented with two Glenfiddich Food & Drink awards.

Through a glass darkly

IF 23 million pints of beer are supped in Britain a day, and most of them come from the 750-plus brewers operating within these shores, and if real ale in all its multifold styles is enjoying a glorious resurgence in pubs across the land, then surely British brewing is in splendid shape for the coming decade. We can all look forward to CAMRA's 50th birthday celebrations being be an even more jubilant affair than this year's hearty shindigs.

Up to a point, Lord Copper. Or to put it more bluntly, wishful thinking, I'm afraid. Yes, it's true exciting things are undeniably afoot in the beer world. And beer is still by some way the biggest alcoholic drinks category of them all. But it's equally true there are ominous developments being played out that could yet put a serious damper on that golden ale anniversary in 2021.

Consider the harsh facts of beer life over the past few years. Pub beer sales are at the lowest level since the Great Depression of the 1930s, despite a 36% increase in the population. Total beer volumes are down nine million pints a day, or 11 million barrels per year, since their peak in 1979; and beer volumes in pubs are down 16 million pints a day over the same period, or nearly 60%. And the fall has been accelerating: in the past decade alone, beer volumes in pubs are down 20%. Overall, and despite the lurid media picture of uncontrollable binge drinking, we've actually been consuming less alcohol each year since 2004.

Through a glass darkly indeed, and the statistics are just as sombre for pubs themselves, the bastions of beer. Since 2005, their numbers have fallen from 59,000 to perhaps as low as 52–50,000 – estimates vary – but a terrible toll has been taken by the recession on the Great British Pub, particularly its community brethren, which make up three-quarters of all our pubs.

Whereas even as recently as 20 years ago, it was through pub handpumps that the vast majority of beer used to flow, the supermarkets have put a stop to that. They exploited their vast buying power to beat up brewers and market beer as their great loss-leader. Peddling it below-cost ('with the ethics of drug dealers' in the words of one senior medic), they now retail over twice as much beer as pubs. Total alcohol sales used to reflect the dominance of the pub in the nation's drinking habits: in these past two decades, the on-trade's share has plummeted from 75% to 25%.

Many cultural and economic factors can be evoked to explain what has happened to our national drink, but tax policy has been one of the most decisive factors. The beer-duty escalator, which has driven up beer duty by 2% above inflation for the past few years and will do so for three more yet, has created a 40% beer duty increase in the past three years alone. Government now makes 50 times more profit on a pint than do the national brewers. Beer tax in Britain is eight times higher than France, ten times higher than Spain and 11 times higher than Germany.

While beer's share of all alcohol sold in Britain has been falling from 70% to 40%, wines, spirits and cider have enjoyed a far more lenient tax regime. Regional cask brewers, for example, are taxed at twice the rate per pint paid by Britain's largest cider brand.

The tax hikes have hit the on-trade far harder than the off-trade, where supermarkets have had the muscle to force brewers to absorb the rises themselves. The subsequently vast price disparity between the cost of beer in pub and supermarket has encouraged home consumption of alcohol.

In the face of these depradations, brewers and publicans have lobbied exhaustively for a more even playing field, but without success. Many commentators believe the government has a secret agenda: its duty rises are an undeclared health policy aimed at driving down alcohol consumption. That would make more sense than their stated aim of raising revenues, for as duty has risen, so tax take has fallen.

After years of failing to persuade the Treasury of its arguments, it's unlikely we'll see a more favourable duty regime any time soon, though a tax break for beers of up to 2.8% abv was offered this year as a token gesture, and a desire expressed to persuade EU regulations to extend this to 3.5%.

Minimum pricing has been regularly touted as the most effective way to curb supermarkets' alcohol strategy, but government is nervous of a full-blooded assault on such a powerful sector (and one which helps fight inflation). Until it commits itself to a ban on below-cost selling, which includes the cost of production, pubs and brewers will continue to lose out.

Pubs have responded to the increases, and to their many competitors for the leisure pound, in ways that have not necessarily helped beer. The favoured way to the pub customer's heart in recent times has been through the stomach, particularly since the 2006 smoking ban, and Mitchells & Butlers has led the way. Over 900 of its 2,000 outlets (one can no longer call them all pubs) are heavily focused on food, and the company has plans to extend this to all but 100 of them. 'A business like M&B has got to break out of the mentality of thinking of itself as a pub company,' chairman John Lovering told the *Financial Times* in March last year. 'We want it to start thinking like a licensed catering company.'

Others are following hard on their heels, though with some reservations that will please traditional pub lovers. Marston's chief executive Ralph Findlay explained to the *Publican's Morning Advertiser* in June this year: 'In the past five to six years, we've moved food in our managed pubs from 25% to 41% of take, and it will be 45% in three years. I'm not sure I'd want to push it further. The restaurant sector is very competitive and you have to differentiate yourself. We do that by being a pub.'

Food also draws people who are not regular pub visitors – women and families and older people, who are clearly important targets if the pub is to widen and secure its future customer base. So successful has food proved that a Mintel survey last year showed more people now go to the pub for a meal than a drink. The danger here for pubs is that pub-goers associate the pub with going out for a meal rather than a drink with friends, and as diners tend to go to the pub less frequently than drinkers, the longer-term effect could be fewer pub visits. This would further accelerate the fall in the amount of pub alcohol, and particularly beer, that's consumed.

After such tales of unremitting gloom, it's time to turn to recent developments that offer more hope for the next decade. And there are several which do suggest better times for beer, or perhaps more accurately certain types of beer, may still be possible. Of these, the real ale revival, with its profusion of choice and diversity, is the most positive beer trend for many years, though we must tread with caution. Overall cask sales in recent years have actually been static – because the internationally-owned brewers have given up on their national brands so thoroughly in favour of lager that their lost volumes have taken until now to be equalised by the regional and micro brewers, even though they have been strongly out-performing the beer market. But now, at last, it can be said with confidence, total real ale volumes are starting to rise.

Cask currently makes up 15% of all on-trade sales, and remains the only 'USP' pubs possess. Mintel research shows that 20% of customers select their pub on whether it serves cask ale. As well as the myriad micros, brewers such as Moorhouse's, Timothy Taylor, Hall & Woodhouse and Adnams have all invested significant sums in their breweries recently, intent on growing future sales. With 50% of customers never having tried real ale, and nearly half of all pubs not serving cask, there seems plenty of potential for growth.

It's that which undoubtedly prompted Molson Coors to swoop on the successful Cornish brewer Sharp's earlier this year, setting off alarm bells across the cask market. Global brewers have shown scant interest in cask for decades, engineering $142 billion worth of international deals in the past five years instead, and some ale lovers fear a wave of regional and family brewer takeovers.

While there are bigger fish to fry – and the $70 billion acquisition of SAB Miller by Anheuser-Busch InBev is currently being mooted, while SAB makes a $9.5 billion move on Foster's – 50,000 barrel cask breweries must seem very small beer indeed. However, economic history suggests consolidation of the global brewing industry (and it appears to be reaching an end game) will inevitably at some stage focus attention on whatever successful brands remain outside their control. Globals rarely create brands; they acquire them, then maximise their cost structure. Britain's family brewers could never compete on efficiency grounds with the globals' production facilities: their shareholders might find the overtures hard to resist.

Should they ever fall into the hands of a global brewer, some British brands, notably Fuller's London Pride, would have their international prospects bolstered. But there are not many of our bottled beers with substantial overseas fan clubs , so the globals would be scrapping over market share in Britain.

For all the real ale purists' visceral disdain for these global 'lager louts,' it would be fascinating to see what might happen if they got behind real ale and promoted it intelligently. An oxymoron to many, perhaps, but Heineken's ownership of Caledonian, for example, has been good for Deuchars. And the Dutch giant is now looking to offer free trade customers a far wider range of ales than ever before.

How might British customers react if their favourite real ales were owned by multi-nationals? A hard core of drinkers might boycott their favourites, but the majority of drinkers would probably be far less concerned as long as they still taste good. Heresy? Possibly, and it's true that provenance, history, localism are all issues that play well for real ale currently. But then again, Old Speckled Hen has hardly suffered a consumer backlash since Greene King re-rooted it to Bury St Edmunds.

National/global brewers might well be tempted to go further down this route if the power of the pubcos was ever to be broken. Commenting on the ongoing Parliamentary Select Committee examination of the tie, Deutsche Bank analyst Geof Collier has remarked that the international brewers would see the end of the tie 'as a fantastic opportunity to recover margin.' As he points out, they've been on a losing streak since the Beer Orders, with pubco power lording it over them, which has meant depressed margins and therefore little opportunity for investment and innovation. If the politicians choose to crack open the market, it could lead to some very interesting opportunities for a more exciting beer market in Britain.

When the only innovation we've seen in a long time is super-chilled beer, and bottles that indicate when they're cold enough to drink, that is certainly long overdue. And marketing commentators say consumers are more adventurous these days and are bored with big brands. They're looking to experiment and seek choice of beer, in their pubs and in their supermarkets. Graeme Craig, Sales and Marketing Director at Shepherd Neame, believes consumers no longer define themselves through 'big-ticket items such as the largest fridge freezers or foreign holidays, which are now easily available to everyone: they're more interested in associating with issues like organics and fair trade, recycling and localness. Food and drink definitely plays a far bigger part in how they view themselves, as does their connection with their community, which all play well with regional brewers like ourselves.'

He also detects a 'flight to quality' and a more discerning consumer palate, with an interest in different styles of beer for which there's a willingness to pay a little more. 'But consumers don't necessarily see the pub as providing that. It's a real challenge for pubs to work much harder in engaging with their customers.'

Some pubs are already extremely well attuned to these needs and are offering beers that are genuinely distinctive and offer a real point of difference. John Roberts, who has recently stepped down from running Fuller's beer company for many years, has been impressed by the range of beers at the Euston Tap, near Euston Station. And particularly by the extensive range of interesting keg beers, drawn from the US, Europe, Australia and many other parts of the world, as well as lagers from England. 'These keg beers are distinctly superior and make the mass brands like Foster's seem very dull by comparison.' The Rake pub/bar at London Bridge sports an even more extensive range of beers, and is constantly packed out with discerning drinkers.

So far, this is an urban phenomenon, catering to more adventurous drinkers, but many British brewers are trying to work out how far it could go, and looking anxiously at their own more limited portfolios. The extraordinary rise of the micros has posed them a major challenge. In the face of their popularity, Greene King is starting to reverse its previous stance and allow its tenants and licensees to sell a selection of locally-brewed micro beers. Another way to respond would be to embrace and encourage foreign craft brewers into their pubs. Clearly, these would be keg beers not real ales, but they are stimulating great interest among discerning beer drinkers. However, if pubs can use new beers, wherever they come from and whoever might own them, to bring new consumers to the party, then our brewing and pub trade might be in a far better state in ten years than many dare imagine today.

ANDREW PRING is the former editor of the *Morning Advertiser*, weekly paper of the pub trade, and is a former chairman of the British Guild of Beer Writers.

Ian McMillan

Three Marvellous Beer Haiku:

Forty beery years!
Raise my glass to the sunlight,
The foamy pint-light.

Look: without CAMRA
We'd have Watney's Red Barrel
And guts like treacle.

Four decades of ale:
A lake we can all dive in
And come up singing!

IAN McMILLAN is a poet, broadcaster
and comedian. His programme *The Verb*
is broadcast on BBC Radio 3 and he is
poet-in-residence at Barnsley football
club and English National Opera.

Books for Beer Lovers

Good Beer Guide 2012

Editor: ROGER PROTZ

The *Good Beer Guide* is the only guide you will ever
need to find the right pint, in the right place, every
time. It's the original and best-selling guide to around
4,500 pubs throughout the UK. Now in its 39th year,
this annual publication is a comprehensive and
informative guide to the best real ale pubs in the UK,
researched and written exclusively by CAMRA
members and fully updated every year.

£15.99   ISBN 978-1-85249-286-1

Good Bottled Beer Guide

JEFF EVANS

A pocket-sized guide for discerning drinkers looking
to buy bottled real ales and enjoy a fresh glass of their
favourite beers at home. The 7th edition of the *Good
Bottled Beer Guide* is completely revised, updated
and redesigned to showcase the very best bottled
British real ales now being produced, and detail
where they can be bought. Everything you need to
know about bottled beers; tasting notes, ingredients,
brewery details, and a glossary to help the reader
understand more about them.

£12.99   ISBN 978-1-85249-262-5

BOOKS

300 Beers to Try Before You Die!
ROGER PROTZ

300 beers from around the world, handpicked
by award-winning journalist, author and
broadcaster Roger Protz to try before you die!
A comprehensive portfolio of top beers from
the smallest microbreweries in the United
States to family-run British breweries and the
world's largest brands. This book is indispensible
for both beer novices and aficionados.

£12.99   ISBN 978-1-85249-273-1

Great British Pubs
ADRIAN TIERNEY-JONES

Great British Pubs is a celebration of the British pub.
This fully illustrated and practical book presents
the pub as an ultimate destination - featuring pubs
everyone should seek out and make a visit to.
It recommends a selection of the very best pubs in
various different categories, as chosen by leading beer
writer Adrian Tierney-Jones. Every kind of pub is
represented, with full-colour photography helping to
showcase a host of excellent pubs from the seaside
to the city and from the historic to the ultra-modern.
Articles on beer brewing, cider making, classic pub
food recipes, traditional pub games and various other
aspects of pub life are included to help the reader truly
appreciate what makes a pub 'great'.

£14.99   ISBN 978-1-85249-265-6

The Book of Beer Knowledge

JEFF EVANS

A unique collection of entertaining trivia and
essential wisdom, this is the perfect gift for beer
lovers everywhere. This second edition includes
more than 200 entries covering everything from
fictional 'celebrity landlords' of soap pubs to the
harsh facts detailing the world's biggest brewers;
from bizarre beer names to the serious subject
of fermentation.

£7.99   ISBN 978-1-85249-292-2

London's Best Beer, Pubs & Bars

DES DE MOOR

London's Best Beer, Pubs & Bars is the essential guide
to beer drinking in London. This practical book is
packed with detailed maps and easy-to-use listings
to help you find the best places to enjoy perfect pints
in the capital. Laid out by area, find the best pubs
serving the best British and international beers
wherever you are. Features tell you more about
London's rich history of brewing and the city's
vibrant modern brewing scene, where well-known
brands rub shoulders with tiny micro-breweries.
The venue listings include a variety of real ale pubs,
bars and other outlets with detailed information on
opening hours, local landmarks, and public transport
links to make planning any excursion quick and easy.

£12.99   ISBN 978-1-85249-285-4

The History of CAMRA DVD

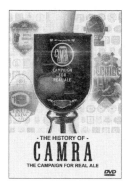

The Campaign for Real Ale is one of the largest and most successful consumer rights groups' operating in the UK today but it wasn't always that way...

Learn about the birth and early years of CAMRA in this riveting documentary, which is packed with archive material provided by CAMRA members, and interviews with the people who were there. The film charts the Campaign's inception on a holiday in Ireland, its growth through the 1970s and early 80s, and the evolution of CAMRA into the industry-shaping organisation it is today.

Featuring contributions from CAMRA's founders, past and present members of the National Executive, politicians and representatives from the brewing industry, this is a must-own DVD for anyone eager to get in touch with CAMRA's 40-year history.

The documentary's director David Rust said:

'The story of CAMRA is one that deserves to be told – A real David and Goliath tale. Hearing these people speak first hand about their experiences was a privilege and I know that CAMRA members both old and new will enjoy watching it as much as I have making it.'

The *History of CAMRA* DVD is available for just £9.99.

Order these and other CAMRA books and products online at **www.camra.org.uk/books** (overseas orders also taken), ask for our books at your local bookstore, or contact: CAMRA, 230 Hatfield Road, St Albans, AL1 4LW. *Telephone* 01727 867201

A Campaign of Two Halves

Campaigning for Pub Goers & Beer Drinkers

CAMRA, the Campaign for Real Ale, is an independent not-for-profit, volunteer-led consumer group. We campaign tirelessly for good-quality real ale and pubs, as well as lobbying government to champion drinkers' rights and promote local pubs as centres of community life. As a CAMRA member you will have the opportunity to campaign to save pubs under threat of closure, for pubs to be free to serve a range of real ales at fair prices and for a reduction in beer duty that will help Britain's brewing industry survive.

Enjoying Real Ale & Pubs

CAMRA has over 130,000 members from all ages and backgrounds, brought together by a common belief in the issues that CAMRA deals with and their love of good quality British beer. From just £20 a year – that's less than a pint a month – you can join CAMRA and enjoy the following benefits:

Subscription to *What's Brewing*, our monthly colour newspaper, and *Beer*, our quarterly magazine, informing you about beer and pub news and detailing events and beer festivals around the country.

Free or reduced entry to over 160 national, regional and local beer festivals.

Money off many of our publications including the *Good Beer Guide*, the *Good Bottled Beer Guide* and *CAMRA's Great British Pubs*.

Access to a members-only section of our national website, **www.camra.org.uk**, which gives up-to-the-minute news stories and includes a special offer section with regular features.

Special discounts with numerous partner organisations and money off real ale in your participating local pubs as part of our Pubs Discount Scheme.

Log onto **www.camra.org.uk/joinus** for
CAMRA membership information.

CAMPAIGN
FOR
REAL ALE

Do you feel passionately about your pint? Then why not join CAMRA

Just fill in the application form (or a photocopy of it) and the Direct Debit form on the next page to receive three months' membership FREE!*

If you wish to join but do not want to pay by Direct Debit, please fill in the application form below and send a cheque, payable to CAMRA, to:

CAMRA, 230 Hatfield Road, St Albans, Hertfordshire AL1 4LW.

Please note that non Direct Debit payments will incur a £2 surcharge. Figures are given below.

Please tick appropriate box	*Direct Debit*	*Non Direct Debit*
Single membership (UK & EU)	☐ £20	☐ £22
Concessionary membership (under 26 or 60 and over)	☐ £14	☐ £16
Joint membership	☐ £25	☐ £27
Concessionary joint membership	☐ £17	☐ £19

Life membership information is available on request.

Title _____ Surname _____ Forename(s) _____

Address _____

_____ Post Code _____

Date of Birth _____ _____ _____ E-mail address _____

Signature _____

Partner's details (for Joint membership)

Title _____ Surname _____ Forename(s) _____

Date of Birth _____ _____ _____ E-mail address _____

CAMRA will occasionally send you e-mails related to your membership. We will also allow your local branch access to your e-mail. If you would like to opt-out of contact from your local branch please tick here ☐ (at no point will your details be released to a third party).

Find out more about CAMRA at **www.camra.org.uk**   *Telephone* 01727 867201

*Three months free is only available the first time a member pays by Direct Debit

CAMPAIGN
FOR
REAL ALE

Instruction to your Bank or
Building Society to pay by Direct Debit

DIRECT
Debit

Please fill in the form and send to: Campaign for Real Ale Ltd. 230 Hatfield Road, St. Albans, Herts. AL1 4LW

Name and full postal address of your Bank or Building Society

Originator's Identification Number

9	2	6	1	2	9

To The Manager   Bank or Building Society

Address

Postcode

Name (s) of Account Holder (s)

Bank or Building Society account number

Branch Sort Code

Reference Number

FOR CAMRA OFFICIAL USE ONLY
This is not part of the instruction to your Bank or Building Society

Membership Number

Name

Postcode

Instruction to your Bank or Building Society
Please pay CAMRA Direct Debits from the account detailed on this Instruction subject to the safeguards assured by the Direct Debit Guarantee. I understand that this instruction may remain with CAMRA and, if so, will be passed electronically to my Bank/Building Society

Signature(s)

Date

Banks and Building Societies may not accept Direct Debit Instructions for some types of account

DIRECT
Debit

This Guarantee should be detached and retained by the payer.

The Direct Debit
Guarantee

- This Guarantee is offered by all Banks and Building Societies that take part in the Direct Debit Scheme. The efficiency and security of the Scheme is monitored and protected by your own Bank or Building Society.

- If the amounts to be paid or the payment dates change CAMRA will notify you 10 working days in advance of your account being debited or as otherwise agreed.

- If an error is made by CAMRA or your Bank or Building Society, you are guaranteed a full and immediate refund from your branch of the amount paid.

- You can cancel a Direct Debit at any time by writing to your Bank or Building Society. Please also send a copy of your letter to us.

detached and retained this section